What Others are Saying:

"The name alone of Yanni's new book conjures up visions of infinite possibilities that reside within us. *Magical Keys: Creating Miracles in Your Life* takes you by the hand and shows you that peace of mind is just a thought and a breath away. In the tradition of master teachers, Yanni not only gives you the tools to peace and success, but shows you how to use them. Make sure you have a copy of this magical volume on your bookshelf."
— **John Harricharan, award-winning author of the bestseller,** *When You Can Walk on Water, Take the Boat*; http://www.spiritual-simplicity.com

"When Yanni speaks in person, he radiates a gentle quietness that is immediately recognizable. Reading *Magical Keys* is a lot like speaking with him. From the pages of his book you'll get some of the same profound stillness.

[*Magical Keys* is] engagingly written.... I couldn't put it down...

I highly recommend *Magical Keys*. Read it. Read it again. Underline and highlight. Give copies to anyone you care about at all. But the most crucial point - do explore meditation for yourself. Then, all the way to your core, you'll begin experiencing the serene kind of power that Yanni describes here."
— **Charles Burke, author of** *Command More Luck* & *Inside the Minds of Winners*
http://www.BullsEye-Living.com

"There is a place within each of us where the waters are calm, the sweetness of spring blossoms fills the air, and birds sing with uncommon splendor. It is a magical place of understanding, of healing, and where miracles are routine. *In Magical Keys to Self Mastery: Creating Miracles in Your Life,* Yanni Maniates teaches us how to find this special place. He shines light on the path that will lead ordinary lives to extraordinary happiness."

— William E. Hablitzel, M.D., author of *Dying Was the Best Thing That Ever Happened to Me: Stories of Healing and Wisdom along Life's Journey;* http://www.dyingwasthebestthing.com

"*Magical Keys to Self Mastery* is a simple, yet elegant, clear, easy to read and understand guide to bringing the joys of meditation, intuition and the "path of the heart" into your life and into the life of your loved ones and children. Few have the wisdom and gentle ways that distinguish Yanni Maniates.

Loving husband, father, teacher of intuition, meditation and Self-Mastery and baseball coach, Yanni lives his life in the same way he writes; with warmth, simplicity, compassion, kindness, passion and always in alignment with the wisdom and joy of his soul. This book is a must-read for the student of meditation or intuition. Do yourself a favor and get a hold *Magical Keys.* You will be giving yourself a great gift!"

— Susan Barbara Apollon, PA Licensed Psychologist & Author of *Touched by the Extraordinary,* http://www.touchedbytheextraordinary.com

"If you want peace, Yanni Maniates shows you the path. He masterfully guides you to connect with the divine experience of both yourself and others. Yanni's book, *Magical Keys to Self-Mastery* is both heartfelt and practical."

  —Terri Marie, award-winning author of *Be the Hero of Your Own Game*
  http://www.herobookonline.com

"This is a very enlightening book for spiritual growth and manifesting miracles in your life. Use the keys that Yanni gives you, have FAITH and TRUST that they will open the door to greater happiness, joy and success in all areas of your life."

  —Greg Tharpe, Author: *THE GODSEND - How to Create Heaven in Your Life*
  http://www.thegodsendbook.com

"What a treat to discover this book!

I am fortunate to have met Yanni and his family while attending a conference in Washington DC. Being in Yanni's presence is immediately calming, and his spirit is one of love and service. The wisdom contained in this book is a vast and endless treasure you will want to read many times, as each reading will net you a new understanding.

As you come to experience Who You Really Are, your fears and worries will evaporate, and you will understand that all is well.

Thank you, Yanni, for such an insightful and inspirational message."

  —Holleay Parcker, author of *Using Intuition in Real Estate*

MAGICAL KEYS
TO
SELF-MASTERY:

Creating Miracles in Your Life

⚫————————⚫

✳ Yanni Maniates ✳

Mentor with the Masters® Press

Magical Keys to Self-Mastery:
Creating Miracles in Your Life

Published
by
Mentor with the Masters® Press

Yanni Maniates, 520 Stevens Road,
Morrisville, PA 19067

First Edition

ISBN-13: 978-0-9794564-0-4
ISBN-10: 0-9794564-0-1

Library of Congress Control number: 2007902063

The Life Mastery Institute
Be free, Be joyful, Be nourished
(215) 295-5444
Email: *yanni.maniates@verizon.net*
Web Site: *www.LearnMastery.com*
Blog and Podcasting Site: *www.LifeMasteryBlog.com*

Acknowledgements

I would most especially like to thank my wife, Jaime, for all
her encouragement, insight, love and support;

our son, Sean, master teacher of joy and
living in the moment;

for all my friends and students for helping
me find my Self;

Philip and Vivien Burley for all the wisdom and love
they have shared so freely with us over the years;

and John Harricharan, for being such a sage, kind and
generous master teacher and mentor.

The winds of grace are blowing all the time.
you have only to raise your sail.
Sri Ramakrishna

Seek truth in meditation, not in moldy books.
Look in the sky to find the moon, not in the pond.
Persian proverb

*Meditation is the **key** that*
opens you up to your Soul.
Yanni Maniates

Table of Contents

Foreword

Nearly thirty years ago a Tibetan Buddhist monk I had come to know said to me "When you meditate do you meditate with or without images?" I turned to him and said, "Meditate? What's that? I don't meditate." As we continued our walk, he explained that meditation was fundamental to his life and he told me something of his practice of meditation. I said to myself, "I think it's about time to learn something about meditation." Thus began a journey that has continued to this day.

That journey might have been different had I had this wonderfully useful book, *Magical Keys*, that you now hold in your hands. Yanni Maniates is a gifted teacher of the way of meditation, what he calls "learning how to create a life of internal mastery and mindfulness."

In these gentle, practical and insightful chapters he leads us step by step into the world of self-mastery and meditation, ancient traditions that have taken many different forms and employ many different techniques throughout the history of humankind's religious and spiritual journey. There are Buddhist, Christian, Taoist, Hindu, and Native American – to name but a few – ways of meditation and self-mastery, and other ways that have no names.

Though techniques vary and teachings often employ the distinctive languages of the varying traditions, they agree that mastery/meditation is not about differences of doctrine or of technique but about joyous even magical "being." Yet, paradoxically, we need to learn how to "be."

That is why these pages are so useful: they teach us a way of "being." As Yanni says "learning to meditate, quiet my mind and touch the deep place of peace within me is the greatest skill I have ever learned to improve my life." Here he shares his learning with us.

The *Magical Keys* that we encounter here are non-sectarian but grow out of the wisdom of many traditions. They take us into that "peace of mind" that Yanni says is but "a breath away," "a thought away." He teaches us a way that allows us to "create miracles in our own lives." He guides us to the "heart of listening" – "the most important skill the one can develop."

Yanni has provided a road map to help us find our way back "home" to the special temple of our own soul so that we might drink of its riches. There is nothing here that has not been tested in the most important crucible: one's own life. There is only wise guidance into a way of self-mastery and meditation that can enhance and empower one's life and lead it into that realm of peace and well-being that is the greatest treasure of every life.

> *M. Darrol Bryant, PhD*
> author of *Religion in a New Key*
> Professor of Religion & Culture,
> Renison College, University of Waterloo

Magical Keys to Self-Mastery:
Creating Miracles in Your Life

Introduction

Is it possible to manifest miracles in your life? Is it possible to live the life you want to live and to be who you want to be?

Of course it is! But you must first come to know who you _really_ are and what you _really_ want in order to actualize it. And to do that you need to have the keys that will help you to do it.

This book gives you solid, easy to apply, proven tips and techniques on how to really get to "know yourself" from the "inside out." In this way you can bring greater joy, passion, purpose, creativity and love into your life. This book is a primer on Self-Mastery and on how to make your life miraculous.

The first chapter **Peace of Mind is a Breath Away: The Fine Art of Meditation** gives you an in-depth introduction to Meditation, explains why it is the foundational key for all change, growth and miracles in your life and offers a simple meditation exercise to help you get you started. Meditation introduces you to your "most significant other"---yourself!

The second chapter **Peace of Mind is a Thought Away: As You Master Your Thoughts, You Master Your Life** explains how important it is for you to be conscious of your thoughts, how they create the experiences you have in your life, and how to master your thoughts so that your life is an expression of the deep joy and passion that lies within you.

The third chapter **Using Meditation to Relax and Manage Stress** explains the deleterious effects excessive stress can have on you and offers a couple of simple, easy to implement meditation exercises that help you to relax and bring greater health and happiness into your life.

The fourth chapter **Life Is a Trip, But Where Are You Going? The Art of Choosing "Who to Be" Rather Than "What to Do"** offers suggestions on how to create real quality experiences in your life by learning how to simply "be" instead of always "doing." Instead of always creating "to Do" lists, here you learn how to create a "to Be" list. It is through this process that you can create miracles in your life.

The fifth chapter **Meditating with Your Children: Relaxation, Communication, and Quality Time for Your Family** teaches you how to incorporate meditation into the rhythms of your family life so that you can vastly improve the overall quality of your life and the quality of your children's lives. Here you learn how to make everyday life sacred and miraculous.

The sixth chapter **The Art or "HeArt" of Listening** helps you to learn how to "listen" from "within" rather than from "without."

True "listening" is not an active, assertive state. It is not a state that judges, understands, or analyzes. It is simply a state of "being," a state of silence, a state of openness, receptivity, and allowing. It is quiet and still and does not pay attention to words or appearances; instead it senses the "essence" of things. It looks into the Soul of people, experiences and all things. It is a state of simply being present and just "knowing."

By learning how to "listen" one can truly experience the full wonder, mystery and majesty of oneself and of all of life. This chapter opens one to this kind of true "listening."

The seventh and final chapter **A Time of Collective "Initiation"** is a brief reflection, from an internal perspective, on what is happening on the global scene during these times of great transition and uncertainty.

As well, I have included a section of some of my favorite quotes on Self-Mastery and Meditation, a Postscript, and a brief section about my work.

Lastly, I have added a bonus booklet entitled: *Magical Keys to Self-Mastery: Creating Miracles in Your Life,*

Meditation Booklet. In this booklet you get the verbatim transcript of four guided meditations that are based on meditations that I have outlined in the book.

Practicing, and even just reading through, these meditations will help you to best integrate and absorb the message of *Magical Keys.**

Life is meant to be "magical." Claim the "magic" and the mystery of it all and then "live it!"

Wishing you all the best! Peace be with you! It is your birthright!

* I have recorded these full-length meditations (forty-eight minutes worth). If you would like information about acquiring them, please email me at: yanni.maniates@verizon.net

CHAPTER ONE

Peace of Mind is a Breath Away: The Fine Art of Meditation

L earning to meditate, quiet my mind and touch into that deep place of peace within me is the greatest skill I have ever learned to improve my life.

Meditation is the art of self-mastery, of learning to experience each moment with calm awareness and compassion with regard to oneself and others. It is learning how not to identify with all of our many thoughts and feelings, but choosing instead to identify with the profound peace that dwells within us and that is what is left behind when we stop compulsively thinking.

Meditation is the art of paying attention,
of listening to your heart.
Rather than withdrawing from the world, meditation
can help you enjoy it more fully, more effectively, and
more peacefully.

Dean Ornish, M.D.

Meditation is the art of learning how to tend
the sacred ground of your life.
It connects you with your inner world.
By meditating you learn how to care for
the garden of your mind.
First, you learn to identify what is growing there.
Then you learn how to nurture
and plant what you want
and weed out what you do not want.

Yanni Maniates

This place of peace, this state of meditation, is available to all of us. It is not something only a "select" few can attain. It's not as if some of us got the "meditation gene" and others did not! It is a natural ability we have—freely given to us all.

Unfortunately no one has ever provided us with an "owner's manual" for our minds, so we are not aware of this incredible potential within us. Meditation is actually the process that helps us develop our own "owner's manual" for our mind.

Meditation is an opportunity to sit quietly and spend "quality time" with our most "significant other," ourselves. It is an opportunity to come to "know thyself;" and in coming to "know thyself," one is better able to appreciate, heal and love oneself.

Meditation is an opportunity to connect at the deepest of levels–with our soul, our higher self, and to tap into our highest natural potential. When we meditate we touch in with that part of us that has great wisdom and creativity and is connected to infinite love, peace and potential.

I can assure you that when you connect with that pure place of peace that dwells within, even for a second, you will be hooked on this "sweet ambrosia of the gods." And you will want to go back as often as possible to access that refreshing, revitalizing essence of peace that is at the core of your being.

So, meditation is the art of learning how to identify or interact with that peaceful center within. It is accomplished by not getting caught up in our fears, worries, anxieties, responsibilities, etc. It is done by quieting our minds and opening our hearts. This allows that peace at the center of our being to flow into our awareness unimpeded by our negative thoughts and feelings.

When we are not all "clogged up" with negative thoughts and feelings, when we empty ourselves of them, we allow stillness and peace to flow in and fill us up. We then enter a state of joy, peace and love that is so liberating.

Meditation teaches us how to be our true selves—how to be in this state of enduring peace. It is an antidote for the over emphasis we find so prevalent today on always "doing" and "thinking." As Deepak Chopra said, we are meant to be human "beings" and not just human "doings" and human "thinkings."

We are meant to spend quality time with ourselves on an ongoing basis so that we can get to know who we truly are. We can't do this, if we are always on the go, always doing and thinking, never having any quiet time for ourselves and with ourselves. As you get more and more into meditation, the benefits of what I am describing will become clearer to you.

So, the goal is inner simplicity–maintaining a quiet mind in the midst of a busy, hectic life.

Why, you might ask is it worth maintaining a quiet, balanced mind. The answer is: A tense mind creates a tense body and a stressed out life; a relaxed mind creates a relaxed body and a healthy happy, life.

There are numerous scientific studies that show the direct link between stress, illness and longevity. [See chapter 3, *Using Meditation to Relax and Manage Stress*, for more information regarding this aspect of meditation.]

So, meditation helps to put us into a new relationship with our thoughts and feelings, a healthy one. But meditation is not something you can just read about and gain any benefit from, you must sit and practice it in order to enjoy its numerous benefits.

There are many meditation techniques that can help to quiet the mind and help us to experience a true, lasting peace. Observing the breath is one of the oldest and most accessible and powerful methods. It is used by beginners and masters. It is often the first technique that is taught. So, I would like to offer you a simple meditation exercise you can do for about five minutes anytime in the day.

Start by setting a clear intention that you want to spend quiet, quality time with yourself. Then sit with your spine comfortably upright, without being rigid or tense. Relax your jaw. Let it be slightly open. Close your eyes. Let your arms be relaxed and place your hands on your thighs or in your lap. Let your feet be firmly on the floor. Or, if you have the flexibility, by all means, sit in the traditional yoga posture on the floor. You can achieve a very profound state either way.

Now, while breathing in and out of your nostrils, focus your attention on your abdomen. Let your belly comfortably expand on the inhalation and contract on the exhalation. Don't strain. Be as relaxed as possible. As you do this, count your breaths. See if you can count ten full breaths without getting lost in your thoughts. If you lose track, don't worry, just gently go back to counting your breaths again.

Count each inhalation and exhalation as one full breath. Do this for at least ten full breaths. By doing this a couple of times a day, you will begin to notice a major difference in how you feel.

Please note that you can also do this exercise with your eyes open, for example, while you are standing in a line, waiting for a bus or an appointment, in a meeting where you don't have to be fully focused, and you can even do this while driving your car.

Yes, just keep your eyes open and focus on your breath and the rise and fall of your abdomen and then just count your breaths. After just a few minutes of doing this you will be pleasantly surprised at how balanced, relaxed, attentive and grounded you feel.

So, constantly use your breath as an ongoing frame of reference or "ground" for your being. Whenever you get lost in compulsive thinking or in "doing" too much, come back to an awareness of your breath.

Your breath is always in the present and if you focus your attention on it, it will calm and slow you down. You *can* stop yourself from "past-tripping" and "future-tripping." Just come back to your breath, calm down and get grounded.

We waste an enormous amount of our precious energy worrying about the future and reliving the past. Use your breath to come back to the present and revive your energies. And then use these energies to create joy and success in the present and to plant seeds for even greater joy in the future. This is the way to peace of mind. There is nothing more grounding and centering than your breath.

Peace of Mind really is only a Breath Away.

So, remember, meditation takes practice, but everyone can do it. It is not easy, at first, for us to learn how to calm our minds, focus our thoughts, and concentrate on our inner worlds. But with patience and practice one can experience an incredible leap forward in the quality of one's life.

The hardest part of beginning a meditation practice is just beginning. Forget all the reasons not to. Just start today, be patient, and enjoy! You'll never regret it!

As **Rousseau** said:
Patience is bitter, but its fruit is sweet.

Chapter Two

Peace of Mind is a Thought Away: As You Master Your Thoughts, You Master Your Life

————————————————————————————————————— ∾

Our thoughts are our only "real" possessions. For wherever we go, whatever we do, they are always with us. They either uplift and inspire us or they burden us with negativity and heaviness.

In this chapter I would like to explore the role of thought in our life and how powerful our thoughts and their subsequent emotions really are.

Usually, most of us barely pay any attention to what we are thinking. We spend more time choosing the clothing we wear, the food we eat, the car we drive, than we do choosing the thoughts we have.

> *We are what we think.*
> *All that we are arises with our thoughts.*
> *With our thoughts, we make the world.*
> *Speak or act with an impure mind*
> *and trouble will follow you*
> *As the wheel follows the ox that draws the cart...*
> *Speak or act with a pure mind*
> *And happiness will follow you*
> *As your shadow, unshakable.*
> **From the opening verses of The "Dhammapada,"**
> **a collection of the Buddha's teachings**

Yet, our thoughts have a profound influence on us. How we feel, how we act, what we attract or repel in our life is wholly the result of the kinds of thoughts we "choose." In fact, all the experiences that come to us in our life, every circumstance, relationship, possession, "luck" (good or bad), indeed everything that comprises our daily experience, is a result of the predominant thoughts we hold and the feelings that accompany those thoughts.

How is it that our thoughts and feelings create what we experience in our lives? It is because of a simple universal law: *"like attracts like."* What this means is that we attract experiences that are of a similar vibration to our predominant thoughts and feelings. Let's look at an illustration of how this works.

Suppose you want to have more prosperity in your life. Perhaps a flood of very large bills has unexpectedly come in; the car needs a major repair, or even worse, to be replaced; or you might feel a desperate need for a vacation welling up inside. You are very keenly aware of what you most want in your life now: "more money."

Keeping in mind the law that "like attracts like," there are basically two ways to think and feel about this topic. If the person in this example feels negative about her circumstances, focusing upon the lack of money: "I never am able to pay my bills." "Something always goes wrong with my finances." "No matter how hard I try, I can never get ahead," etc., a negative signal is sent to the universe.

Since "like attracts like," what will she attract: money or the lack of it? The universe hears this familiar "moneyless" signal, strong and clear; and it responds with more of the same: more unpaid bills, more financial difficulties, still no new opportunities to get ahead, etc.

On the other hand, if this same person, after becoming aware of her desire for more money, begins to imagine how wonderful it would feel to have all the bills paid; imagines the nice, soft hum of a new car while driving down the road; and fantasizes feeling deeply rested while sitting on an exotic beach, she would begin to attract a totally different experience.

Again, since "like attracts like," she would have begun to send a new signal to the universe: one of plenty and abundance. *In time*, <u>bit by bit</u>, she would attract the people and circumstances that would allow for what she is dreaming of: all the bills paid for, a new car, a relaxing vacation, and more of the joy and ease she desires.

What is amazing about this process is that it doesn't matter whether our thoughts are being chosen deliberately and consciously, or whether they are "selected" by "default" in a habitual, mindless, unexamined way. They affect us in the same manner.

In the end, conscious or not, we are the creators of our experience. The universe will deliver to us whatever we want. But we cannot ask for a particular thing to come into our lives while we, at the same time, believe we can't have it. It doesn't work that way. We can't say I want a new, red BMW convertible, and at the same time lament that we can't afford it.

The way we feel in any moment is the result of the thoughts we have chosen to dwell on. If we could send the universe a pure signal of what we really want, both in thought and feeling, our life experience would be a much closer match to our desires.

The way we feel or "vibrate" is our point of magnetic attraction. The universe does not hear our words; instead, it feels our vibration and sends us more of the same, either positive or negative. What is important to remember is that the thoughts we think create an "energy signature" or vibration around us; and, over time, this vibration sets into motion the kinds of experiences we have.

As human beings, we have been given this incredible gift called "life." This gift of "life" gives us access to an unlimited supply of pure, positive universal life force energy. Our ability to think is the mechanism by which we summon this life force to us and then "mold" it into whatever we want. We "mold" the energy with the kind, quality, and intensity of the thoughts and corresponding emotions we have. With each thought and feeling we choose, we begin to attract and create something.

So, negative emotions are actually an early guidance system that let us know we are "mis-creating," so to speak. In other words, in that very moment of negativity, our emotions are signaling to us that we are currently focused upon thoughts which are drawing into our life the opposite of what we really desire. Therefore, our feelings are a very important barometer that we need to carefully monitor.

When we stay stuck in negative thoughts, we restrict the flow of the pure, positive, creative life energy that is constantly streaming to us from the universe. So, just as our bodies would respond negatively to the restriction of oxygen, our lives and spirits respond negatively to the restriction of this pure positive energy when we are caught in negative thinking.

We *can* control how much pure positive energy comes to us by the way we think. We *can* learn to master this powerful energy and be masters of our lives.

Let's look at another example to illustrate this point. Suppose you want very much to develop a loving relationship with someone, but somehow you can never seem to get it to happen. If you honestly examine your thoughts about this subject, you will, for sure, find that you have thoughts that oppose your desire for companionship: i.e., feelings of being unworthy of love, feelings that your freedom would be restricted, etc.

But know that these thoughts, no matter how habitual and deeply ingrained, can be changed. As they are *faced* and seen for what they are, then *embraced* and accepted, they can gradually be *replaced*, thus bringing about the desired change.

The bottom line is this: you cannot expect to receive what you want when the way you feel deep, down inside is its opposite. When you feel unworthy of love, you cannot attract a companion; when you feel poor, you cannot attract prosperity; when you feel overweight, you cannot attract slimness; when you fear illness, you cannot attract health.

Yes, your habit of getting stuck in thoughts is years old; and habits can be quite tenacious. Yet, you *can* learn to gain mastery over your thoughts. This can be done simply by cultivating a constant awareness of how you feel. For when you realize that you are feeling "off," it is a sure sign that your thoughts are "off," too, and that you are attracting into your experience what you do not want.

So, to change this feeling, trace back and determine what thoughts created the feeling. Then *gradually* change your thought pattern from a negative one to a positive one. This will then change your vibration. And *in time* you will manifest what you really want.

It is only by slowing down and observing your patterns of thoughts and feelings that you can ever escape the prison of your old beliefs and fears. Then you can learn to develop new patterns, thus manifesting new experiences that are a closer match to what you really desire. Begin with the smaller issues in your life and in time you will also be able to handle the "biggies."

Each moment need not be a repeat of the past, but instead can be a moment of new creation, of new beginnings, of incredible richness and potential. So, learn to listen to your feelings; they will definitely give you very reliable feedback on what you are thinking and therefore creating.

This is the art of self-mastery — the art of mastering life. What so few people realize is that we are capable of choosing the thoughts we think, and, therefore, attracting experiences that make life "good." Though we may believe, at times, that our thoughts "think" us, they do not. We can and <u>do</u> choose our thoughts.

You have the power and ability to create a whole, new life for yourself — a life of joy, freedom, peace and more. Just claim it!!!

Know that *Peace of Mind is just a thought away*; it is a choice you can make in any moment. And so too, are beauty, love happiness, joy, power, wisdom, all just a thought away! Be patient and loving with yourself and in time you will succeed.

As *Michelangelo* said about the beauty of his statue David:

He was there all the time; he just had to be freed.

And as **Thich Nhat Hanh,** the Buddhist Mindfulness meditation teacher wrote:

There is no path to Enlightenment,
Enlightenment is the way.
There is no path to Peace
Peace is the way.
There is no path to Happiness,
Happiness is the way.

CHAPTER THREE

Using Meditation to Relax and Manage Stress

Stress is an everyday fact of life. You can't avoid it; but you can manage it in a way so that it works for you and not against you. If you allow stress to run unchecked, you will most likely create problems for yourself physically and emotionally.

Below is a list of some of the various kinds of ailments that chronic stress can cause:

Muscle weakness, muscle tension, shoulder, neck, and backaches

Hypertension

Peptic ulcers, stomachaches

Colitis, constipation, chronic diarrhea

Amenorrhea–suppression of menstruation, failure
    to ovulate

Impotency and loss of libido

Asthma, bronchitis and other respiratory ailments

Diabetes

Decalcification of bones, osteoporosis

Inhibition of immune and inflammatory systems

Headaches, fatigue

Arthritis

Premature aging

Depression

Anger, hostility

Difficulty making decisions and concentrating,
    frequent crying

Insomnia

Please note that when you are overly stressed, your adrenal glands secrete corticoids (adrenaline, epinephrine, and norepinephrine) which inhibit digestion, reproduction, growth and tissue repair, and the immune and inflammatory responses.

So, as you can see from the above, chronic stress is not good for you. But, just as we get so caught up in a chronic stress response to life's challenges; we can also learn how to experience the "Relaxation Response®" through the practice of meditation.

By using meditation, you can significantly lessen your level of tension and experience the following positive, relaxing, scientifically proven effects:

Highly alert and focused mental state

Deep state of relaxation

Decrease in perspiration, muscle tension, and levels of stress hormones

Slower more even breathing patterns

Slower heartbeat

Lower and more stable blood pressure

Diminished fight or flight response

Better digestion

A boost in energy, stamina, and natural immunity

Speedier recovery from illness

Improved response time, motor skills,
    coordination, & other physical responses

Enhanced mental concentration

Greater emotional mastery and stability

Enhanced feeling of well-being

Prevention of physical problems

More graceful aging

Better sleep

**As well, the regular practice of meditation can help
with the following conditions:**

Lessens the frequency and severity of asthmatic
    attacks and other allergic reactions.

Materially reduces stress and stress-related
    illnesses like heart disease, hypertension,
    tachycardia, headaches, and insomnia.

Significantly alleviates present moment and
    chronic physical pain from arthritis, back
    injury, and most other causes.

Also, meditation can help with: Fibromyalgia, Chronic Fatigue, Diabetes, Gastrointestinal Disorders, Sexual dysfunction, Post-traumatic Stress, and Panic Attacks.

So, as you can see, you can significantly improve the quality of your life by learning how to incorporate meditation into your life. Meditation techniques are simple, short, and easy to do. And they will help make your life so much more enjoyable.

[Please note that it is advisable to consult a medical professional if you have any of the above-mentioned conditions.]

Breathing Exercises

Improper breathing is a common cause of ill health.
Andrew Weil, M.D.

What follows is a description of a series of simple breath meditation exercises that will help you to calm your emotions and be so much more relaxed:

Emotional Distress: When you are under emotional stress, breathe into your abdominal area and keep your focus of attention there. Let your belly comfortably expand on the inhalation and slightly contract on the exhalation. Breathe in for a count of four, hold briefly, while you imagine any tension or negativity being gathered into the breath, and then breathe out all the tension and negativity for a count of four or more.

Use this breath to help calm yourself when you are feeling anxious, overly excited, or worried, as well as when you are doing something new. Do at least ten of these breaths. It helps to calm you down and re-energizes your adrenals, pancreas and digestive organs.

Feeling Overwhelmed: Breathe as above, but now into your heart area. Just notice the rise and fall of your breath in the heart area. It is more subtle than in the abdominal area, but still perceptible.

Use this breath when you feel overwhelmed, overworked, overloaded, suppressed, depressed, fearful, lacking in confidence, in a crisis, under pressures, etc. This energizes the heart and lungs.

Mental Tension: Breathe into your head, as above. Consciously take a deep breath high up into your nose and try to feel the energy circulating in your head, face, eyes, neck and throat. Breathe oxygen into your brain and head, neck, face, eyes, neck and throat. Feel energy flow into all these areas.

This breath is for headaches, dizziness, migraines, insomnia or when you feel mentally foggy and unclear.

Preventing Tension: In order to prevent excessive tension from building up and creating distress, you first need to be conscious of what is going on in your body and mind. So, regularly and consistently take the time during the day to observe yourself and be aware of how your body and mind are responding to the situation at hand.

If you are feeling the effects of stress, catch yourself before it gets any worse and start releasing the pent up energy by breathing consciously. Just being conscious like this will go a long way in helping you not hold on to any negative energies.

So, when you feel tension, just use any or all of the three breathing techniques I have taught you above and you will feel so much better. Doing at least ten full breaths like this will help to calm you down and/or re-energize you.

I would suggest that you practice these simple techniques at least five times a day. It will only take a few moments of your time. If you do, you will feel so much more relaxed and at peace than you ever imagined.

Peace be with you!

A significant number of people who think they have serious heart disease are almost certainly actually suffering from breathing disorders.
Sheldon Saul Hendler, M.D.

CHAPTER FOUR

Life Is a Trip, But Where Are You Going? The Art of Choosing "Who to Be" Rather Than "What to Do."

Whenever I mention to people that I teach stress management, meditation, and life mastery skills, they almost always say to me, "Boy, do I need that!"

We live in a very fast-paced world. Information, opportunities, and challenges are expanding exponentially every day. Life is full, to say the least!

Too often, our experience of life is like a series of breathless, unconscious, one-after-the-other chase scenes in a fast-paced movie. Rather, I believe life is meant to be a series of vibrant still shots or landscapes, to savor and enter into with just a sprinkling of the right amount of madcap scenarios to add some spice.

Often, as soon as we wake up in the morning, we are immediately mentally inundated with an infinitely long "to do" list. Instead, I would propose that we start off our day by focusing on creating an exquisite, rich, high-quality "to be" list.

As I see it, it's not about what you want to do today that is most important, but rather, what you want to be, or feel, or experience. What qualities of life do you want to primarily participate in today: peace, balance, love, courage, happiness, joy, humor, harmony, confidence? Or do you really want to go into a lowest-common-denominator default mode and experience their opposites?

Why not begin your day by jotting down the quality that you would like to experience and embody that day? Then, as the day progresses, create various practices that will help you to remember and reinforce that quality so that your day is filled with what is *really* most important to you and with that which will bring you the greatest lasting value.

For instance, you could choose feeling "peaceful" as the most important "to be" quality for a particular day. Therefore it would be with peacefulness that you would want to begin, follow through with, and end every activity and interaction in your day.

In other words, let the quality you want to experience be more important than the list of goals you want to accomplish. Wherever you are, whatever you are doing, and with whomever you are doing it, always ask yourself, "How can this interaction be permeated with the quality I have chosen today?"

Here is a technique, one of many I have developed and taught over the years, which can help you to refocus on your quality again if you realize that you have lost it.

First, slow yourself down; next, take seven deep breaths. As you breathe in, imagine that you are breathing in the quality that you have chosen for that day; see and feel it permeating your whole body-mind, and then, on the exhalation, see and feel its opposite being expelled. Really feel it and see it as you breathe in deeply and gently. At the end of these seven breaths you will feel refreshed and on target again.

Just trust that as you learn to be consistent with focusing on your quality, you will be surprised that you not only have the pleasure of experiencing the positive quality you have chosen, but as an added bonus, you also find that what was most important on your "to do" list has been accomplished easily and effectively.

Note that what I am suggesting you begin practicing here is an "art," and sometimes, when you first sit down to create a work of art, things can get quite messy. Don't be discouraged if at times you lose your vision and just can't seem to be able to keep your chosen quality in focus. In time you *will* get better at it.

In time, as well, you will learn that if you do lose your focus, it doesn't really matter! When you do lose it, first, just notice that you have lost it, and then, with a sense of humor, have a good laugh at yourself, give yourself a break, and when you have calmed down, gently come back to practicing the quality you have chosen.

So, when you wake up in the morning, why not begin with your "to be" list, and then, let the quality that you have chosen permeate your whole day. To help you stay focused, do the breathing exercise described above as often as you can remember; do it while you are driving your car, standing in line, waiting for someone, etc. Also, some people find it helpful to put Post-it® notes up everywhere, with the quality written on them as reminders. You can even write your quality on the palm of your hand or automate a message on your computer.

Just imagine, after a year of practicing this, how rich and full a tapestry of qualities and experiences you will have woven into the fabric of your life and into the lives of your loved ones, as well as many others. I know many people who have turned their lives around practicing this simple approach!

It *is* possible! Give yourself a chance; you deserve it. You won't always do it perfectly, but it's never about being perfect, is it? It *is* all about the journey and not the destination.

Remember, you can always, every day, in every moment choose "to be" filled with a wondrous joy, peace, and love. It is a choice, and it's *yours*. You are a human "being," not a human "doing!" Begin your day by putting first things first: claim your mastery and step into and experience who you want "to be" today!

Learn 'not doing' and everything will fall into place.
Lao Tsu

*you've got to come out of the
measurable doing universe
into the immeasurable house of being*
e.e. cummings

CHAPTER FIVE

Meditating With Your Children: Relaxation, Communication, and Quality Time for Your Family!

H ad we had enlightened parents who would have taught us how to meditate when we were children, our lives would have been so much richer; our life choices so much sounder, and so much more in line with our real talents and passions. But, alas, many of us were not so blessed. Yet we can provide this for our children. As Crosby, Stills, Nash, and Young encouraged the 60's generation, we can "teach our children well." We can provide them with an invaluable tool to assist them in the art of "living well."

First and foremost, it is through meditation that we can nourish in our children a sense that they are never alone, that they are always in loving company, and that they can always find an embracing feeling in their hearts. As a parent, this is the most precious gift we can bestow upon our children and the foundation upon which "living well" can then become the prevailing note of their lives.

As well as instilling a feeling of love and well-being in our children, meditation has many practical benefits. Meditation can help your children sleep better; develop better concentration skills, which can result in improved school and athletic performance; enhance their creativity and self-image; and help them to learn how to quiet themselves and deal better with their anxieties.

In addition, teaching our children how to meditate creates a wonderful opportunity for us as parents to ignite, rekindle and/or deepen our own practice of meditation. As well, because meditation helps us to relax and open up our hearts, it allows us to spend real "quality time" with our children, rekindling and/or deepening our relationship with them.

So, how can we begin to introduce this precious gift of meditation to our children?

First of all, introduce meditation as a fun, joyful time for the whole family, as an opportunity to be relaxed, creative, and spontaneous together.

Second, it is very important to develop a regular practice and to make it a natural, integral part of the day. So, set aside a specific time when the whole family can regularly meditate (such as after dinner or just before bed) and pick a quiet room where everyone can be comfortable. Do it consistently and joyfully, starting off with just a few times a week, then gradually building up to doing it daily or almost daily.

Remember though, that in any situation, getting a child to cooperate is not always the easiest thing to do; but, by being consistent in your own meditation practice and lovingly persistent with your child, most children will over time eagerly join in. If on any particular day a child is unwilling to meditate, give her/him the choice of doing another quiet activity. Eventually, you will see that they will choose to meditate, more often than not.

Note, too, that the regular daily family time for meditation can be extended to include time for sharing feelings and ideas and for ironing out problems and developing trust. After meditating, you will be surprised at how much easier it is to express oneself sensitively and openly and how much less complicated it is to find a solution to a family "problem."

What follows is a brief outline of how to introduce meditation to children of different age groups.

For infants and children up to two years in age, the primary goal is to get them to learn how to sit still. We can do this by sitting quietly with them for a few minutes and just tuning into our breath or into them with no other thoughts, no other distractions. By doing so, just for a few moments, we are helping them experience a quiet, peaceful time with us. Our goal here is simply to model a time of quiet for them.

Even as they get more active and pass through the "terrible twos," we can still spend a few moments with them teaching them how to be quiet. Most children can handle one or two minutes of quiet time at this age. Chanting AUM or just listening to or singing a soothing lullaby with them can be a great way to introduce quiet time to a child. My wife and I did this with our two year old, a very active child I might add, and he actually looked forward to it every night.

When your child reaches the age of three, you can begin to introduce actual meditation exercises and even expect them to stay focused for a few minutes— even one minute is enough. The child can be taught to chant AUM with you or perhaps chant the name of a religious figure. As well, he/she can be led through the following exercise:

Have the child sit cross-legged or in a chair with their back comfortably erect. Have them close their eyes and breathe in and out through their nose slowly, counting to four on the in breath, then holding the breath for a count of one or two, and then exhaling for a count of four. Have them take about ten breaths like this.

Then have them imagine that they are safely floating on an emerald green lake in a light blue boat on a stack of cream-colored pillows. On each inhalation the boat rises slightly and on each exhalation it falls ever so gently. Have them coordinate their breathing with the image and sensation of floating in the boat.

Then to bring them out of the meditation, have them first focus on their toes, then their feet, their calves, their thighs, their torsos, their hands, their heads and finally their breath. Then guide them to open their eyes with a soft focus, so much more relaxed and at peace than when they began.

Start with a minute of this exercise and gradually build to a few minutes. If the child is very tense on a particular day, have them first tense and release different parts of their body beginning with the face and then moving down to the toes. Then do the above meditation. Or just start by giving them a gentle one or two minute massage before you begin the meditation.

For children six to ten years of age, more self-discipline can usually be expected. After some practice, they can be expected to meditate at least five to eight minutes a day, but please do not force anything on them. The following exercises are appropriate for children in this age group. Use what I offer as a guideline for what they can do, and then use your own creativity to come up with a variety of other fun things that your children might enjoy.

Have the child concentrate on a watch or clock with a second hand and have him focus on the dial going around the clock. Instruct him not to let anything distract him — any noises, thoughts, etc. See how long he can do it. Even keep a progress chart. The same exercise can be done by looking at a candle flame, a flower, a tree, etc.

As well, you can do an exercise that is an extension of the lake relaxation one above. After the child has become relaxed by doing the floating in the boat exercise, have her now imagine that she is barefoot at the top of a staircase. The staircase is thickly carpeted in a color of her choice. Have her begin by putting one foot down after the other as you slowly count her down 10.....9.....8.....7.....6.....5..... 4.....3.....2.....1. Now at the bottom of the staircase there is a door. When she opens the door and walks inside, she walks inside her heart.

Have her explore what it feels like to be in her heart, physically, and then, emotionally. Then have her ask her heart a question, internally–not out loud. Then give her a moment or two to listen, sense or see an answer. Then gradually bring her out of the meditation by having her become aware first of her feet, her legs, her torso, then her arms, and finally her head.

If she would like, have her discuss her experience and feelings. With all these exercises you can play some calm background music, if you wish.

For children eleven to fifteen years of age their minds are really beginning to develop as is their ability to truly reason and discriminate. They are capable of longer periods of concentration depending on how adjusted and emotionally balanced they are. For most, this is a very turbulent period. Spending "quality time" with them is of paramount importance during this time in their lives. Try the following meditation with them.

Begin by having them do the breathing and lake relaxation exercise. Then lead them in this tree meditation: Imagine you are a tree, you are one with a tree. Feel that you are deep inside the center of a tree, the tree is your body. How does it feel? (pause) .... Now feel your roots burrowing deep into the earth (pause) ...., now feel the bark as part of your body (pause)...., now feel the sap running through you (pause) ...., now feel all of the branches as part of you (pause) ...., now feel all leaves as part of you (pause)...., now feel the breeze gently rustling your leaves and the sun warming you (pause)...., now feel a bird's nest in your branches (pause).... Feel all of this life running through you and around you (pause).....

Then slowly bring them out of the meditation as above. You can do similar exercises with the wind, water, fire, a bird, the soil, a flower, etc. This exercise can last any where from five to fifteen minutes. After this, discuss their experience with them and their feelings about it. Let the discussion be free flowing.

Children older than fifteen can be led in the same meditation exercises that adults do.

So, it is easy to begin to incorporate meditation into your family life. It does not take up too much time, and it gives you something to focus on in your "quality time" with your children. Be assured, meditation will deepen the trust and openness of your relationship with your children, and it will help them enormously in developing greater self-reliance, creativity, concentration, happiness, self-awareness, health, and a stronger, more positive self-image.

It will also help them be more in touch with their feelings and know how to most appropriately express them. And, finally, meditating with your children will bestow these same wonderful "gifts" upon you. *So, why not begin today?*

By meditating with our children we help them to see the world through their *own* eyes and to experience it with their *own* hearts. In this way, we are teaching them to live their lives fully. We are teaching them to truly come to "know themselves" and to "be true" to themselves. By doing so, we are cultivating many precious "gifts" and skills within our children and are, in so doing, truly "teaching them well!"

CHAPTER SIX

The Art or "HeArt" of Listening

Listen, Listen, Listen to my Heart's Song.
Listen, Listen, Listen to my Heart's Song.
I will never forget you.
I will never forsake you.

Yogananda

Yogananda wrote the song above. He taught his students to sing these words continually as a mantra because doing so would help them to always remember that it is their own voice that is *the* most important to listen to first.*

* For a lovely rendition of this song/mantra, listen to the album *Songs of Healing* by *On Wings of Song* & *Robbie Gass*, Spring Hill Music.

Yogananda was a truly profound spiritual master and teacher. If you have not read his <u>Autobiography of a Yogi</u>, I would highly recommend it. It is one of the classics of spiritual literature. It is a life-changing, inspiring guidebook. Just the act of reading it put me into a very profound state.

Yogananda embodied the archetype of the Nurturer and expressed the spirit of the Divine Feminine in his life, even though he was in a masculine body. And as I will explain in greater detail later, it is through the Divine Feminine energy that we can learn to really "listen."

Listening has many facets. Below is an outline of the aspects of listening that I will be exploring with you:

- ❖ How to listen to an "other." I might say right here at the outset that there is no such "a thing" as someone or something "other" than you. [I'll say more about what I mean by this shortly.]

- ❖ After that I will discuss how to "listen" to nature and the animal kingdom.

❖ Then how to "listen" to Spirit.

❖ Followed by how to "listen" to that part of us called the little self or the ego? That part of us that we often do not want to "own" or acknowledge, that we often wish to disinherit, despite the fact that it is has some very valuable things to say to us.

❖ As well, how to "listen" to our Higher Selves.

❖ And, lastly, how to "listen" to the God/Goddess within.

What is "Listening?"

By the way, there is no **real** separation among these six categories. "Listening" is all the same, but it is helpful to break the topic up in this way in order to make more "sense" of it for you.

*Actually, I hope none of this makes **sense** to you!*

I hope you do not use your mind to understand any of this because it is not with the mind that you hear, listen, or understand anything. Listening is **not** a cognitive function. It is a function of the heart.

Listening is not an active, assertive masculine state. It is not a state that judges, understands, or analyzes. It is simply a state of "being," a state of silence, a state of openness, receptivity, and allowing. It is quiet and still and does not pay attention to words or appearances; instead it senses the "essence" of things. It looks into the Soul of people, experiences, and all things. It is a state of simply being present and just "knowing." It is a receptive, feminine state.

Listening is the most important skill that one can develop. It is a surrender, a merging with, a communion; it is just being present with no agenda.

PART I

"Listening" to an "other"

So, back to the concept of "other;" there is no "other" as I wrote earlier. One of the gifts of learning to listen is to realize that there is no "other." There is only One; and the only way to "listen" is to merge with or become part of or one with that which you are listening to. There is no other way to truly "listen."

Otherwise, all you are doing is judging and analyzing with your mind, and, by doing so, you *separate* yourself *out* from what you are listening to and experience it as "other" than yourself when it is **not** "other."

This "separating out" is what creates all the conflict within our selves and with "others" and also all the conflict in the world. We see people and things as "other." But really, how can anything or anyone be "other"?

In the Judeo-Christian tradition there is the event called "The Fall." From my point of view that event describes the time when we chose to stop "listening"

with our hearts and, instead, began to judge with our minds. We ate of the fruit of the "Tree of the Knowledge of Good and Evil," that is, we entered the world of judgment, analysis, duality and separation.

We no longer experienced life from within, but, instead, we experienced it as "other" than us or outside of us. We started judging and analyzing instead of feeling and that created the sense of separation that we feel from our selves, each other, nature, Spirit, our Higher Selves and God/Goddess. This is what cast us out of the Garden of Eden.

Vine Deloria, PhD, a Native American and a scholar so aptly wrote in this regard:

> *For primitive people the presence of energy and power is the starting point of their analysis and understanding of the natural world...primitive people felt power, but did not measure it. Today we are able to measure power, but do not feel it.*

Rene Dubos, celebrated microbiologist and author wrote:

> *Sometimes the more measurable, drives out the most important.*

In our Western cultures we have given preeminence to the cognitive, masculine, ways of knowing and allowed the intuitive, feminine ways of knowing to be ignored. Despite all the valuable technological advances we have created, this over emphasis on the cognitive has wrecked havoc on us physically, emotionally and spiritually. We need to come back into balance again; we need to "come to our senses" so to speak. Thus we can integrate both ways of knowing, and then we can reenter the Garden.

As well, our cutting off of the intuitive way of knowing has significantly limited our ability to experience the wonders of creation and the incredible richness of life.

As *Elizabeth Barrett Browning* wrote:

Earth is crammed with Heaven, if we but listen.

Heaven is everywhere and in everyone. Each one of us and everything that we could possibly interact with is simply an entryway, a mirror, a portal to Heaven, to our Higher Selves and to the God/Goddess within if we could "listen" to it, if we could "see" or really "feel" it.

Everyone and every experience is a manifestation of the God/Goddess within. Every one and every thing is the divine, immortal **"You"** or **Thou**. There is no "other." If we could learn again to "listen," we all could reenter that Garden and find our Selves.

The following brief dialogue from *Theophane the Monk's*, <u>Tales of a Magic Monastery</u> I feel best sums this up:

> *"Father, could you tell us something about yourself?"*
> *The Monk leaned back.*
> *"Myself?"' he mused.*
> *There was a long pause.*
> *"My name ... used to be ... Me ....*
> *but now ... it's You."*

Listening to an "other" is a skill that so few of us have.

So, listening to an "other" is a skill that so few of us have. We have a young son who is a dear, wonderful soul. Once in awhile when we are under duress and are impatient, we find ourselves saying to him, "Now listen to us, Sean; be a good listener, ignore your feelings. It is only what we feel or want that matters."

What we are saying here is: "Sean, do what we want you to do. Do not listen to yourself. Right now, it is inconvenient for us to have you be present with yourself. Be present with what we want you to do and not with what you want to do or feel."

We do this infrequently, but we do find ourselves lapsing into this mode at times. We much prefer to listen to him and honor him.

Parenthetically, this does not mean that we do not help him to set boundaries and instruct him in what is appropriate at a particular moment. All I am saying here is that we really want him to know that his feelings are being heard and honored and that they are important. He is important. What he feels *is* important. I'll say more about how essential this is later.

So often we want an individual to be or act in a way that we want them to. Rather than allowing them to be and act as they are and as they want to.

So, what *does* it mean to "listen" to another?

I have found that most us most of time, myself included, are in a place of self-absorption. Therefore, we are not listening. We are so caught up in projecting a certain impression about ourselves or getting our point across or being heard or being "right" that we pay almost no attention to the person right there in front of us.

Listening can not occur when the mind is preoccupied. "Listening" can only occur in the silence and receptivity of the heart. It can only occur when the little self, the ego, the self-absorbed part of us is silent.

As well, we are often so preoccupied with a problem or a train of thought that we pay absolutely no attention to what a person is saying to us. They are talking to us, but we are simply not there! We are off in some other universe. We are literally not present!

Also, what often happens is that we are so full of "*hubris*" or false pride that we just want to hear ourselves talk and we are not interested in what another has to say. We are not there to listen, we are only there to make another see or hear us; all we want to do is to be externally validated.

This happens because we have a lack of real Self-confidence, that is, we lack confidence in our Higher Self and lack an understanding of what our Higher Self is and who we *really* are; and are, instead, trying to build up our little self's self-confidence, that is, our ego's delusion of confidence or personal superiority.

By doing this we just keep putting up one barrier of separation after the other. Eventually, it becomes very difficult to bring these walls of separation down in our relationships. This is the cause of all the conflict in the world.

So many people over so many different eras just did not know how to listen nor did they want to. They would claim that God was on their side and that they were in the right and "others" were in the wrong. But as I see it:

> *God is not on your side or my side.*
> *He/She is inside every one of us!*

For myself, I really got to understand this when I was in my early thirties. At that time I became the Executive Director of an organization that planned ecumenical, inter-faith conferences all around the world. The people who attended the conferences were academics in religion and philosophy as well as religious leaders from all over the world. Many very fascinating people attended from all walks of life.

Some of the conferences were as large as 1,000 and some of the events were small groups of twelve to twenty attendees. I did this for about seven years and literally went around the world numerous times doing it.

Here I was in my early thirties and the "head honcho" of the whole enterprise while the participants were at least in their early 40's or all the way up into their 80's. Also, most of them were rather eminent in their communities or even internationally.

So, my position as their junior was clearly to serve them all. I had to make sure that the organizational aspects of the event went smoothly and that they were all well cared for. In addition, I had to make sure that the topics that we chose had thematic coherence and that it all came together smoothly. I learned an enormous amount doing this.

One of the most important things I learned was that I had to be "listening" all the time. I had to be a "good listener." Whether I was running a large meeting or just a small planning meeting; I had to be listening. I had to be listening, as well, to mundane complaints such as someone's room was too small or perhaps the glass of water was not placed correctly on the podium. I had to always be listening.

So, given my age and the position I was in; I **had** to listen. All I did was "listen." As well, when I wasn't at an actual conference or a formal meeting, I was meeting with people at my office or talking on the phone with them. When I was at an event, we would have breakfast, lunch, snack and dinner meetings. When I was on the beach in Maui, Hawaii; I was in meetings. At six in the morning, I was in meetings. At eleven at night, I was in meetings: *Listen, Listen, and Listening.*

As time went on I began to see that there were three kinds of people that I was listening to. First, there were the "holier than thou eminences," as I called them. When they talked about the paper they wrote, or their tradition, or themselves, it was all ego; it was all "look at how great I am! Look at how much better I and my tradition are!"

The second group of people was incredibly brilliant intellectually and had wonderful things to say, but they were only interesting up to a point. After awhile

what they were talking about would give me a bad
headache or a severe case of mental diarrhea. They
were so caught up in their heads. They were the
"talking heads."

Lastly there were the Buddhist monks and other
wonderful souls like them who came to these events
simply to enjoy themselves and to enjoy the company
of others. They just laughed and smiled and greeted
you warmly all the time. They were there just to enjoy,
to listen, to learn, to just be present.

I soon began to realize that it was so much more
enjoyable being with those who were present and
listening. Those who were constantly talking about
how great they were or how brilliant their intellectual
theories were, got rather boring; and, interestingly,
those same people **never** asked me a question about
myself. I did not exist on some level other than as a
sounding board. I was truly "other" than them.

But it was these "laughing Buddha" types who would
not only ask me about me, but they would "listen." I
just felt embraced by them. I felt "one" with them.

Even though it was 1985 when I left this position, still
to this day, there are a dozen or so of these "laughing

Buddhas" I still communicate with. [By the way, many of these people were Westerners!]

In order to really be listening one must be silent.

I really learned through all this that it was so important for me to be silent in order to really be listening. It did not matter whether I was in a planning meeting discussing practical things, in a conversation pondering profound issues or just hanging out. In order to hear, I had to be still and listen quietly. It was only by doing this that I was able to hear and respond from a place of connection.

It was not that I did not speak up at times, I did; but I learned not to talk a lot in these settings. I chose to listen. I learned to just be present and just witness what was going on. I learned to go beyond words and appearances and sense the "essence" of the interchange.

I listened in the silence and to the silence, not only to my own silence, but also to the silence between their words. And it was there that I got to "know" them. It was there where I got to know who they really were and what they were really saying.

It was from this place where I could make a comment that would move the discussion into an area that was more productive; or I could sense that the interaction was going nowhere and I knew that it was time for me to excuse myself. I was not judging them, but I could sense when their energies did not match mine.

I learned not to "lean into" conversations or situations where I did not belong and which did not serve my Highest Good or the Highest Good of all concerned.

Too often when we interact with others, we are not listening, we are not present; we are not silent. So, we get caught up in a draining interaction, or we get caught up in our own self-absorption and we miss the opportunity to commune on a heart to heart level with someone. We walk away feeling drained or empty instead of being uplifted.

What also happens is that some people often initiate an interaction because they need energy. They are in the interaction solely for the purpose of draining energy from someone, usually unconsciously. I call these kinds of people "parasites." Not a very nice way to describe someone, yet we all do it at times. And we all have certainly experienced feeling totally drained after a conversation.

If you are not at first quiet and listening silently, you will not know what is going on energetically in an interaction. You will not know whether you are about to be significantly drained or uplifted.

But if you are silent and are really listening, you will realize whether an interaction is for your Highest Good or not. You will know whether the interaction is an enmeshed, stagnated and mutated one or not. This is not meant to be a judgment of that individual, but it is just an objective appraisal of the energies.

At this point, if you are "listening," you can make a decision about whether you want to continue to engage in this interaction or not. If you are really listening, then you can really sense where the interaction is going energetically. You then can make a choice to be with that person's energy or choose not to be with their energy.

It is within this silence that you can know what they are really saying, what the real issue is. Often what someone is saying out loud has nothing to do with what is really going on inside of them.

If what they are saying is energetically off and you are conscious of it, then you can offer a comment that comes from your heart that makes them stop and take notice. Then, if you have said the right thing, all of a sudden, it is as if the spirit that possessed them is gone and now you find yourself in an uplifting interchange.

What is most important here is that you did not take that energy into yourself and get engaged in a whole sequence of negativity and then wonder why afterwards you felt so awful. But if you are not really "listening" from within, you are not going to realize what kind of energy soup you are in and then after the interaction is over you will find yourself wondering why you feel the way you do.

If we are not engaged in a truly "listening" mode, we create the conditions for conflict to arise because we are not paying attention, have no idea what is being said and are not honoring the person speaking. In this non-"listening" mode, we perceive ourselves to be "other" than the person we are talking to. From this left brain dualistic perspective of separation we see someone or something outside or "other" than ourselves and therefore feel justified in ignoring them, "scapegoating" them or even in inflicting physical or psychological harm upon "it."

On the other hand, if we were using our right brain intuitive faculty to listen, we would experience ourselves as "one with" rather than "separate from" an "other" and our response would be quite different and much more embracing and positive. We would better understand the consequences of our actions and words and act more in concert with what is the Highest Good for all concerned.

So, then, how *does* one *really* listen?

You listen by being silent!

How can you have a conversation and be silent, you may ask? Actually, you can have the best ones you've ever had. Let me explain further.

PART II

"Listening" to Nature

How do you communicate or commune with nature? Do you speak English or whatever your primary language is to animals, flowers, or crystals? No way, they do not speak English or any other human language, for that matter! But they do communicate. How? They communicate through feelings and images.

I communicate with our two cats by being still and silent and then just sensing whatever images, feelings, thoughts or perceptions come my way from them. By doing this I get a picture/feeling for what they are saying.

I can communicate in this way, as well, with any aspect of nature. I do not do this by asking, let's say a tree, a question and expecting a computer print out for an answer. The information does not come in a cognitive manner. It comes as a feeling, an image, as an impression. I listen by simply being present and by opening to the energy of the being before me or, in other words, I become "one" with that being.

For example, how did *Edward Bach,** MD discover the *Bach Flower Remedies*? He did not read a book that gave him the information that this flower essence was good for this particular mental state or emotion and that one was good for that one. Rather, he did it energetically; he intuitively connected with the flowers and just "knew."

He used a right-brain faculty and not a left-brain one. He silenced the little ego mind's incessant noise and then he could *really* "listen" to the plants and flowers and a whole system of healing was revealed to him. Yes, he then used his empirical, left-brain to verify what he "felt," but first he "felt" and the later he thought, i.e., used his analytical mind.

Similarly individuals over time in many different cultures have connected with crystals, stones, trees, etc. and have come to understand the healing powers that they embody.

* For more on Edward Bach, MD and his work, see
http://www.bachcentre.com

In effect, by becoming quiet, anyone can connect with the essence or spirit of any "thing" they focus on and "download" all kinds of information about it. You simply go into the silence, open up, and then receive. You come into a "communion" with your object of attention.

This is also true of the indigenous cultures that have created systems that we now use for divination and healing. The Native Americans have created a very precise and elaborate system that describes the "medicine" or "power" that different animals embody.

Now again, they did not read a book to discover this. Yes, they did do visual observations to get a sense for how, let's say, a wolf acts and lives. But what they were doing was so much more than just measuring and judging.

Rather they went into a quiet place and "became" wolf. They became "one" with wolf. By doing so, they, then, "knew" what the wolf's "power" and "medicine" was. And they understood that wolf was "teacher" and what that meant on many different levels.

They did not use words or the left-brain to understand. They used their ability to "feel;" that is, they used their right brain to gather the information. And, again, this can only be done, when the mind (left-brain) is still or quiet. So, over time a very elaborate system or language was created by the Native Americans that connected them very closely with nature.

Language, at best, is a poor form of communication

At this point I feel it would be valuable to offer a few comments about language or words. From my point of view, words or language are very poor forms of communication. They, at best, are pointers to meaning, but they do not express meaning in and of themselves. Actually, they mask real meaning and separate us from it.

Let me explain, the ancient languages were pictographic in nature, Egyptian hieroglyphics, cuneiform, Chinese, etc. and were much better than modern analytical, left brain languages in communicating the essence and subtlety of things because they were pictographic.

I myself majored in Classical Greek as an undergraduate. Though its alphabet is not pictographic, its very elaborate syntax and grammar allows you to easily create pictures in the reader's mind. That is why it was such an excellent language to write great poetry and literature in.

Modern science has come to understand that we store information in our minds as pictures. We do not store information as words. When I say "tree" to you, you do not spell the word "t-r-e-e" out in your mind, but rather a picture of a tree is triggered from your memory and you internally "see" "tree." Actually, you do not just "see" a tree; you actually have an emotion that you associate with the concept of tree that comes up for you, too.

Interestingly, what has happened to us is that we have become a highly analytical, mental, left-brain culture. We think words have meaning in and of themselves, but they do not. All that words can possibly do is point to meaning.

We think we can only understand through analysis, through words and through the "logic" of the left-brain, but that simply is not true. Words make us feel separate from our object of attention and limit our understanding. They objectify all "things" as outside or separate from us.

Whereas the "logic" of the right-brain, albeit different from the left-brain, helps us to see from the inside out and therefore helps us to see the "bigger picture," so to speak. The right brain helps us to feel a part of our object of attention rather than separate from it.

But you can only understand or access the right-brain's "logic" through "feeling" or by silencing the left-brain mind and then in this silence you can become one with the object of your attention. Again, the left- brain only knows how to analyze, judge and categorize which in effect separates you from your object of attention.

It is the right-brain, intuitive faculty that allows us to "see" or sense what is going on from a much broader perspective. It triggers pictures in our minds which give us "the bigger picture," of what we are observing. Remember "a picture is worth 10,000 words;" so a picture communicates so much more than a pile of words ever could. Pictures help us to access the "essence" of a thing.

And, please remember, as I said above, that these pictures that are triggered not only conjure up images, but also emotions. So, we really get to "feel" what we are seeing. Plus, if you let the pictures flow one after the other, they create a movie, so to speak. And then as this movie unfolds before you, you really get into the essence/feel of what you are focusing on.

So, by just focusing on the analysis and judgment of our object of attention, we don't see the whole picture. We get to see only a small portion of it; at best we get to only "skim the surface." But by using our intuitive/listening/right-brain faculty we not only see more of what we are focusing on, but, as well, we get to "see" and "feel" what we are focusing on from the inside out. We get to become one with it and, therefore, come to know it from within. We get to know so much more this way.

PART III

"Listening" to Spirit

Another example to illustrate this point comes from my study and practice of Mediumship. Over twenty years ago I was taking a class on Mediumship. As part of the training we were asked to do intuitive readings for the other members of the class. Before we actually started to "read" for a particular individual he/she was asked to write down the questions she/he wanted to have addressed. The medium, which was me in this case, was not allowed to actually see the questions. All I was allowed to do was to hold the piece of paper with the questions in my hands and pick up on the vibrations.

The first time I tried this, I was very, very nervous and really wanted to know the questions. Why did I want to know the questions? So the little "I" in me could feel safe and secure with knowledge of the question. In this way I assumed I would give the best answer. But that was not what the exercise was all about *nor* was it the best way to get and give the best answer.

I literally thought that I had to know the question in order to give the answer. But that was not true at all. The training I was getting was all about teaching me how to get a feeling about the individual's energy and by doing so I could "tune into" what was really most important for them. It was about using my right-brain to access the information and not my left-brain. It was about becoming quiet and "listening."

It was not about giving an analytical left-brain answer that relied on what I consciously knew. Instead it relied on me tuning into and trusting a deeper and more profound source for the information; a source that would allow me to tap into a wisdom that went beyond my training and my judgments and instead accessed a deeper well of insight that was truly inspired.

So, through this process I learned how to "feel," "sense," and "see" things with my right-brain. I learned to just speak what I sensed/felt/saw *before* I thought about it; and to allow it all to flow out without it being scripted, without any of my left-brain's preconceived notions in the way, without judging or analyzing anything.

I learned to simple watch the movie that was playing in my mind's eye and then speak it out loud. I learned to trust the deeper well of wisdom that wanted to flow through me unimpeded by my preconceived notions. I learned to trust what I felt and saw.

We have all been taught to think before we speak. That went out the window with this training. I learned to speak before I thought. I learned to allow what I said to be inspired and not scripted. And then what I would say could really come from my heart and not from my narrow, analytical mind.

It took a while to get past the point of needing to know what the question was. But now it comes so easily for me and what comes up always amazes me. It's so wonderful to be able to speak from the heart and not the head, to feel first and think later. It makes all things new. It allows for real inspiration and healing to occur.

Another example of what I mean would be helpful here. Recently, I had two people who were good friends come for readings. I read for one right after the other. The first reading was a wonderful, deep, passionate type of reading. I enjoy these the most because they let me open my heart and gush. It was really great.

Then the other person came in and for the first forty minutes all I talked about was her work. It was boring to me because it was not the empathetic "stuff" I like to do. My mind kept saying, "Find something else to talk about." I kept wondering why do I keep going on and on about her work? It was about forty minutes into the reading when she said, "By the way, how did you know that this was all I wanted to talk about?"

So, as it turned out this was exactly what was most important to her. Because of all my training over the years, I knew not to listen to all the "noise" my left-brain was generating, but, instead, to listen to the waves and waves of information that kept coming through about her work.

I have learned through this process to listen to that voice. But if I am not really listening, I am not able to be present for that individual. I am simply not there. I am lost in my head. I am lost in my thoughts and preconceived notions.

A further example relates around our son, Sean. As I mentioned earlier, my wife and I know clearly that in rearing Sean it is so important that we listen to him. It is so important for him to know beyond a shadow of a doubt that what he feels really matters.

Actually, it is *all* that matters.

Also, we want him to never forget to pay attention to what he feels. What he thinks about something or what we or others have taught him to think is not as important as what he feels is important.

We often ask him "what are you feeling?" The most important thing we have learned to do with him is to listen to and be present with him and for him. If we do not let him express or get in touch with his feelings, he will then, in time, deny them. And by denying his feelings, he will be denying his Self; he will not know how to listen to his Higher Self. He will not even know that he has one!

Then he will begin to identify with his little self, which is all the programming, all the scripts that others have given him that he "thinks" he has to play out. Then he will not be him Self. He will be his "little" self. He will be who he "thinks" others want him to be, but not who he "is."

We want him to always remember to ask himself:

"If I am not me, who will be me?"

We want him to be in touch with what he "feels." As Yogananda urged, we want him to listen to *his* "Heart's Song!"

Carl Rogers, the noted psychologist wrote in this regard:

> *Nothing feels so good as being understood, not evaluated or judged. When I try to share some feeling aspects of myself and my communication is met with evaluation, reassurance, distortion of my meaning, I know what it is to be alone.*

When I was my early twenties I went through a dark, existential period in my life where I believed that life was truly meaninglessness and only filled with *angst* and *ennui*. I felt so, so alone.

What I did not realize at the time was that I was not in touch with or listening to my feelings; I was not listening to my Self. I didn't realize at the time that it was only through being in touch with my feelings that I could access my real Self; and by doing so I could, both, *really* find meaning in my life and *never* ever feel alone.

I did not understand that honoring my feelings would lead me to Me, to My Higher Self, to the God/Goddess within. And in this place of connection and "Embrace," I could never be alone. I could only be alone when I identified my "self," with the "little" self, with my ego mind.

This feeling of aloneness or separation is there only because the little self sees itself as separate, as "other than," rather than as connected with All That Is.

One day I finally realized; "Oh my God, I am not 'other.' I am God in finite form who has come forth to embody an attribute of Him/Her in this current, temporary personality. I am a part of the 'One.' I AM that 'One.'"

PART IV

"Listening" to the little self

Now I would like to briefly address how to listen to the little self and why it is so important to do so.

The only way to really listen to your little self is to learn how to sit quietly and meditate. When you sit to meditate, you slow down enough to really hear the incessant noise and static that your ego mind is constantly producing. It usually comes as quite a surprise to hear all of this and realize that it has been going on subliminally for so long.

Many people give up on meditation soon after they start because when they sit down to meditate all they hear is the mental diarrhea that the little self is producing: that is, fear, worry, anger, anxiety, jealousy, etc. And hearing all this they say to themselves: "Oh my God, I'll never change that; it's hopeless. Why bother?" and they give up on meditation.

Yet the only way to get a "handle on your Self" is to sit and listen to all this negative (little) self-talk. For it is only then that you finally realize how insane it all is and that it **must** stop. It is through meditation that one can learn numerous techniques that can help you become a master of your thoughts and mind, a master of your emotions, and, therefore, a master of your life.

We must understand that it is our mind that creates the suffering and tension that we experience in life. Nothing else creates it. Tension and suffering are not created by forces outside of us. They are created by the way we choose to interpret events or people. It is you, totally you, creating and allowing it all! It is your little self responding with fear, anger, and all kinds of dysfunctional programming to the circumstances before you that creates the suffering.

As *Marcus Aurelius* wrote:

> *If you are distressed by anything external, the pain is not due to the thing itself, but to your estimate of it; and this you have the power to revoke at any moment.*

Your Higher Self embraces all experiences, circumstances, and individuals. It sees the Divine Order and Timing in all experiences. It puts all things in the highest perspective and helps you to find the most appropriate attitude and response to it, if you are in touch with it.

So, meditation helps you to access a way to see your experiences through the eyes and heart of your Soul or Higher Self, no longer blinded by the myopia of your ego mind.

So, the gift of learning how to listen to your little self is that:

> One, you first realize how insane it is;
>
> Two, you then realize that you *can and must* change it;
>
> Three, you then learn how to change it by no longer listening to it.

Through meditation you learn to observe what is real and what is just mind "stuff." You learn not to identify with the chaos, static and tension of the ego mind. Instead, you discover the real **You** and find a true, eternal peace that knows no end! You really do!

As *Jack Kornfield* so simply and eloquently wrote:

> *Whatever arises is not Self. It is not I; it does not belong to anybody; it is just conditioning.*

With meditation you learn to realize that you are not your thoughts or your emotions. You begin to realize that what is important is what is "in between" all the thoughts and emotions, namely the Silence. It is in that sacred Silence that you find your Self. It is here and only here where you can listen to an"other" and to your Self.

PART V

"Listening" to your Higher Self

Now, I'd like to discuss who this wonderful being called the Higher Self is? Actually, it/she/he cannot be given a name or a description. But I'll take a stab at it anyhow. I'll let my words be pointers, but remember that they are not ends in and of themselves, just pointers.

I call the Higher Self the "Embrace." For when I feel connected with "It," there is a sense of being totally present with my Self, of being whole and held in the most loving and tender arms ever imagined. It is simultaneously a physical, emotional, mental and spiritual experience and yet it goes beyond all of those, too. It is simply a "knowing" or a "state of being" or a state of oneness.

It cannot be named; it is a state of Grace. The more you choose to listen to it, the more you end up being in its Grace and in its Embrace. It comes in like a gentle, cooling summer breeze and refreshes and fills you to overflowing with a peace that "passeth all understanding."

You then, as Yogananda taught, have learned to "Listen, Listen, Listen to *your* Heart's Song." So, instead of hopelessly trying to develop *self*-confidence, that is, a confidence in your little self, a confidence that can never be stable or strong because it is always looking outside it self for validation; you start to develop a real *Self*-confidence, that is a confidence and trust in the guidance of your Higher Self.

By the way, I would like to add here that there is nothing wrong from a psychological point of view in creating clear, strong boundaries and having confidence in your present personality's identity. Yes, you do need to have a clear sense of identity! But you must realize that this little self's identity is transient and temporary. The only real sense of identity is Self-

Identity and Self-Confidence. That is, learning to identify your self as Self and not as ego/little self.

This is what I have come to understand in my life. That is what I believe Yogananda's song/mantra is pointing to. He is encouraging us to find and to listen to that Self, to *our* Heart's Song. He is saying: "Remember 'that.' Listen to 'that.' Come from 'that.' Dwell in 'that.' Know that 'that' is all there is and that 'that' is all that you really ARE."

You are a beautiful song in the Heart of God/Goddess. Listen to your song! Let your melody be heard! Let it sing your praises!

An anonymous author wrote:

> *You are an emperor not a beggar. You posses the untold wealth of the universe, unimaginable riches. Don't beg for enlightenment, don't plead for it. You are the Self; don't assume that you are impoverished. Give up that yearning and be quiet and the treasure will be self evident as your very nature.*

It is your little self that is asking and begging for enlightenment: "Help! I need enlightenment." No, you don't. You do not need anything. You already *are* enlightenment and you will "know" this when you quiet the ego.

As *Angelus Silesius,* a 17th century mystic wrote:

> *God whose love and joy*
> *are present everywhere,*
>
> *Can't come to visit you*
> *unless you aren't there.*

Translated by Stephen Mitchell in
The Enlightened Heart:
An Anthology of Sacred Poetry

PART VI

"Listening" with Your Heart or Coming to Your Senses

As I begin to come to the conclusion here, I hope that you have not been using your mind to understand any of this. Instead, I hope that you have been "listening" with your heart or your Higher Self. Please do not try to mentally understand the words. In all my classes, I say to my students, please do not listen to a word I am saying, just listen/sense/feel/merge with the energies that are being transmitted.

These energies are being transmitted because of our combined presence and intentions together today. They are not coming from me, by any means. They are actually totally coming to you because of you.

Whatever good you are learning through reading this is because you are listening to your Self and not to me. No person, philosophy, religion or book can teach you anything! They can only act as a catalyst for your understanding, for your remembering! Only you, when you are present to receive the energy that the person, book or teaching is pointing towards, can receive it. And only you can receive it in the unique way that makes "sense" to you.

So, if you are in this state of "being present," if you are in this state of listening, who are you *really* hearing or listening to? You are *really* hearing or listening to Your Self. There is no "other!"

I am making this point so strongly because I want to encourage you to understand that it is so, so important for you not to give your authority away. You are your own author, your own *author*ity. No one else can be that for you.

So, don't ever give your authority away to anyone else. You are wisdom. You embody wisdom. No one else has your wisdom. If somehow someone helps you come to an understanding of some kind, please understand that it is not their wisdom that you now have, it is yours. If someone helps elicit an experience of love in you, that love is yours, not theirs.

They were just a mirror or reflection to you of what was already in you. They were not the source of it. You (i.e., your Higher Self) are the source of your love and wisdom. It resides *in you* and you are rediscovering and uncovering it for yourself. They just help point you in the right direction so you can see it more clearly. They are only a catalyst and **not** the source. They help you to face your Self and see clearly who you ARE.

PART VII

"Listening" to the God/Goddess Within

Lastly, I would like to say a little about listening to the God/Goddess within. I have come to understand or feel that there is no difference between my Self and that which we call God/Goddess.

I realize that for some of you what I have just written may sound blasphemous and for others it may sound rather opaque.

But it is only in the Silence where you can understand what these words might mean. It is you, all along, who have been asking the questions and it is You all along who have been answering them:

*You are speaking to **Your Self.***
*You are understanding **Your Self.***
*You are loving **Your Self.***

You and God/Goddess **are** the same essence. You are the Oneness.

You are, so to speak, a chip off the old holographic block called God/Goddess. You are made in His/Her Image. You are the same "essence."

So, that is why when you truly learn how to "listen" to an "other," you will finally come to really understand or "know" them as Your Self because you will have learned how to connect Soul to Soul, Heart to Heart, Self to Self, Goddess to God.

I believe it is worth repeating *Monk Theophane's* dialogue here again:

> *"Father, could you tell us something about yourself?"*
> *The Monk leaned back.*
> *"Myself?" he mused.*
> *There was a long pause.*
> *"My name ... used to be ... Me ....*
> *but now ... it's You."*

When I learn to see God as my Self, I see you as my Self, too. When I see Goddess/Love in every thing and circumstance, I see every thing, every person, every event and every circumstance as my Self and know without a doubt that all is Good and in Divine Order and Divine Timing.

So, in order to listen to or communicate with an"other" we must become one with them. We must be in "communion" with them.

In this regard it is interesting to look at the etymological root of the word "communion." In Latin "com" means "with" and "union" means "one." So, communion or communicate means "to become one with."

We can't get around it; in order to communicate with or listen to our object of attention we must become one with it. We can not be separate from it and really understand or "know" it. We can not "think" about it and "know" it.

It is in this Silence that you "know" that there is no "other"; there is only You, the Divine You.

William Blake so eloquently summed up what it means to become "one with" your object of attention in the following passage:

> *To see a world in a grain of sand,*
> *and heaven in a wild flower,*
> *hold infinity in the palm of your hand*
> *and eternity in an hour.*

He really "knew" how to listen.

To conclude I would like to end with a few quotes:

Krishnamurti in describing meditation wrote the following:

> *Thought comes to an end. Then there is that sense of absolute silence in the brain. All the movement of thought has ended. It has ended but it can be brought into activity when there is necessity in the physical world. Now, it is quiet. It is silent. And where there is silence, there must be space, immense space because there is no [little] self. The self has its own limited space; it creates its own limited space. But when the self is not, which means the activity of thought is not, then there is vast silence in the brain because it is now free of all its conditioning.*

> *And it is only where there is space and silence that something new can be that is untouched by time or thought. That may be the most holy, the most sacred— may be. You cannot give it a name. It is perhaps the unnamable. And when there is that, then there is intelligence and compassion, and love. So life is not fragmented. It is a whole, unitary process, moving and living.*

As well, an anonymous author wrote:

Silence is ancient. Silence has been in the space you are this very moment for longer than anything else. It will remain after you leave and exist long after all other things have faded.

Lastly, **Thomas Keating** the Trappist monk wrote:

Silence is the language of God.
Everything else is bad translation.

Thank you for "listening!"

To find the way,
Close your eyes,
Listen closely,
And attend with your heart.
Anonymous

CHAPTER SEVEN

A Time of "Collective Initiation"

A number of people have asked me how I see the current series of events on the global scene. So I thought I would share my sense of things, which comes from an internal, non-analytical perspective, with, you, the readers of this book.

This is the time of the **"Collective Initiation"** as Gregg Braden* has written. It is our fears that have created such horrific events and situations, but it is our Love and courage that will heal them.

* *Awakening to the Zero Point: The Collective Initiation;* Gregg Braden; Radio Bookstore Press, Revised edition; 1997.

As best as you can, stay away from fear and keep envisioning the best possible outcome in all situations both global and personal. For if you keep imagining the worst, you add to it and create more of it. If you see the best, then so shall it be.

As well, do not project any negativity on any individuals that you perceive as being responsible for these events. Instead, pray for them and see them surrounded by Light.

The ancient rites of "initiation" were ones in which individuals were put in circumstances where their greatest fears would arise. This was done after they had received extensive training in how to master their minds. For the ancient Masters understood that our reality is created by our pervasive thoughts and feelings; and they knew that the only way to change a fearful world into a peaceful and loving one would be to teach individuals to learn to rise above their fears and projections permanently.

So, in the Ancient Mystery schools one was buried in a sacred sarcophagus (tomb) or a tunnel for three days. If one could master their fears while in this setting, they would live and be reborn. If they succumbed to their fears, then their fears would literally create that which they most feared right there in the sarcophagus and they would be consumed by their own creations.

We are now in the time of the **"Collective Initiation."** We no longer need to enter the solitary sarcophagus or tomb to be initiated into our mastery. Our whole planet is this sacred sarcophagus now. The events transpiring are our **"Collective Initiation."**

We are all in this together. We are not alone.

Go within and connect with the "Embrace of All That Is." There you shall find peace, compassion, understanding, and inspiration. There you will rise above **all** fear. This is what we are all being called to remember and to do.

Please trust and believe that you can do this. Know you have been preparing for this moment all your lifetimes. _**You** are a Master!_ You have the training. The time has come to claim your true inheritance, i.e., to be reborn, to be a Master.

Our collective ability to do this will create a new Reality. The events on the worldwide scene can be a blessing that catapults us all into the "Kingdom of Heaven on Earth" at warp speed; reborn into a whole new reality!

Walk in peace!!! Talk in peace!!! Breathe in peace!!!

Walk in Love!!! Talk in Love!!! Breathe in Love!!! And step aside from any conversations or TV coverage or any exchanges that instill fear. Step away from the fear of those who have temporarily forgotten what the meaning of this time truly is. Step instead into the Light and into your Mastery!

Pray for Peace and understanding! Pray for those directly and indirectly involved! Pray for all the leaders in the world and for the actions they take!

Many Blessings and Much Love! Peace be with you!

Yanni

Symptoms of Inner Peace

Loss of interest in judging other people.
Loss of interest in judging self.
Loss of interest in interpreting
the actions of others.
Loss of interest in conflict.
Loss of ability to worry
(a very serious symptom.)
Tendency to think and act spontaneously
rather than from fear.
An unmistakable ability to
enjoy each moment.
Frequent overwhelming
episodes of appreciation.
Contended feelings of connectedness
with others and with nature.
Frequent attacks of smiling through
the eyes and from the heart.
Increasing tendency to let things happen
rather than make them happen.
Increasing susceptibility to accept
love extended by others as well as
the uncontrollable urge to extend love.

Anonymous

Quotes

Impatience is ignorance of what is supposed to
be happening at the present moment.

Steven Sadlier

We get lost in the past or future,
looking for causes, struggling for solutions.
Until we can rediscover the present moment,
our minds and bodies are stuck in overdrive.

Jon Kabat-Zinn

We don't understand the operations of our minds
and hence we do not operate them very well.

Charles Tart, Ph.D.

I have only three enemies.
My favorite enemy, the one most easily influenced
for the better, is the British Empire.
My second enemy, the Indian people, is far more difficult.
But my most formidable opponent is a man named
Mohandas K. Gandhi.
With him I seem to have very little influence.

Mohandas K. Gandhi

I have a body, but I am not my body. I have emotions, but I am not my emotions. And I have thoughts, but I am not my thoughts. I am something much larger and grander than all of these. I am the master of the vehicle. I am pure Essence which has taken a form in order to experience a life in time and space. I am Spirit, both visible and invisible, with individuality, unique meaning and sacred purpose.

Dr. Roberto Assagioli

When you practice meditation,
slowly the clouds of sorrow melt away.
And the sun of wisdom and true joy will
be shining in the clear sky of your mind.

Kalu Rinpoche

Meditation is a tool for creating both receptivity and stability of mind that our natural wisdom may arise. It is a way of cleansing the mind of all fears and releasing new reservoirs of creativity and energy. In meditation you connect the personal self with the universal Self. You bring your breath in harmony with the great breath. Each time you relax and become more centered, you move beyond the apparent duality of the cosmos.

Diane Mariechild

When you seek anything before stillness, you seek in vain.
Stillness is the road to peace.
You can only find the road with a still mind and
not with a seeking mind.

Barry Long

Today is the tomorrow you were worried about yesterday.
Was it worth it?

Anonymous

I can tell my hand what to do and it will do it instantly.
Why won't my mind do what I say?

St. Augustine

Meditation helps one to acquire an attitude that is deterred by nothing, gains insight from everything, and allows each situation to find its own special good. Then one is like a sapling which, though bent, springs back upright; the water which, though diverted, keeps flowing toward the sea, gradually wearing away all barriers to its course; the grass, which though cut, comes up again if its roots are kept moist.

Robert Ellwood

Be master <u>of</u> mind rather than mastered <u>by</u> mind.

Zen Saying

All of us can work for peace.
We can work right where we are, right within ourselves, because the more peace we have within our own lives, the more we can reflect it into the outer situation.

Peace Pilgrim

Even though explorers spend most of their time lost, they do get there.

Charles Burke

Bless a thing and it will bless you.
Curse it and it will curse you....
If you bless a situation, it has no power to hurt you, and even if it is troublesome for a time, it will gradually fade out, if you sincerely bless it.

Emmet Fox

Keep your face to the sunshine and
you will not see the shadows.

Helen Keller

The only tyrant I accept in the world is
the still small voice within.

Mohandas K. Gandhi

If you want to build a ship,
don't drum up people together to collect wood
and don't assign them tasks and work,
but rather teach them to long for
the endless immensity of the sea.

Antoine de Saint-Exupery

If the only prayer you say in your whole life is
"Thank you," it would suffice.

Meister Eckhart

When you give someone a book,
you don't give him just paper, ink, and glue.
You give him the possibility of a whole new life.

Christopher Morley

Postscript..........

Thank you for reading my book. I hope that it has provided you with bountiful keys that will help you live your life to the fullest.

Life is a wonderful adventure of exploration and growth. When we change the way we "see" ourselves, others and the world, then we can radically change what we experience in our lives. We *can* create the "Good Life" as Socrates suggested—a life that is in harmony with the Truth of who we are and a life that is lived in a state of intentionality, joy, love and clarity.

Rather than slavishly repeating old patterns and problems in our lives because we are caught up in an unconscious, default mode of thinking and feeling, we can instead take the time to "be still" and "listen;" and by doing so we can learn to *truly* hear our Selves. And in hearing and "listening" to our Selves, we can live our lives from a place of enormous authenticity, passion, purpose, love and creativity.

As *Eileen Cady*, the co-founder of the Findhorn Community so eloquently wrote:

> *Cease trying to work everything out with your minds,*
> *It will get you nowhere!*
> *Live by Intuition and Inspiration,*
> *Let your whole life be a Revelation.*

So, put aside some time each day to "be still" and to "listen" to your heart, to your Soul. Take this time to come to "Know Thy Self." **You** <u>really</u> are your "most significant other."

It is so, so important to spend some "quality time" with your Self on a daily basis. If you do, you will find that you truly are a magnificent and majestic being and that you are held in the "Embrace" of the most loving of energies. As well, you will know with a doubt that there is no challenge without a "soul"ution and that everything in your life is truly in Divine Order and Divine Timing.

But you first have to learn to "listen" to that "still, small voice" within. There within you will come face to face and heart to heart with the God/Goddess within that is the essence of who you really are; and then you will "know," without a doubt, that you are "Good" and that there is an intelligent, loving master blueprint that is wisely working itself out in your life right now. It is in this way that you will gradually unravel the magical, majestic, "mystery" and "miracle" of who you are.

> *Life is not a problem to be solved,*
> *but a mystery to be lived.*
> **Thomas Merton**
>
> *I would rather live in a world*
> *where my life is surrounded by mystery*
> *than live in a world so small*
> *that my mind could comprehend it.*
> **Kat Cathey**

If you enjoyed *Magical Keys to Self-Mastery: Creating Miracles in Your Life*, please tell your friends and family. They can acquire their own personal copy at:

www.MagicalKeystoSelfMastery.com or at Amazon.com

Stay tuned for more books and audio products.

Please visit my Web Site for information on the programs and other resources I offer.

www.LearnMastery.com

Also, please visit my blog and podcasting site where every Monday and Wednesday there are written tips (blogs) on Spirituality, Meditation, Intuition and Self-Mastery and on Fridays a weekly audio podcast.

Blog and Podcasting Site:
www.LifeMasteryBlog.com

Also, please feel free to contact me with any questions or comments.

The Life Mastery Institute
215 295-5444
email: yanni.maniates@verizon.net
For information on my meditation CDs:

Peace of Mind is a Breath Away: Breathing Free Meditations

Peace of Mind is a Thought Away: Mastery Meditations

Peace of Mind is an Image Away: Visualization Meditations

Go to:

www.LearnMastery.com/AudioTapesByYanni.htm

Thank you, for joining me. Perhaps we shall meet again. May your journey be filled with all things good and "wonder" full.

Blessings and Peace,
Yanni Maniates

The Life Mastery Institute
Mentor with the Masters® Press
520 Stevens Road
Morrisville, PA 19067 USA
Phone: 215-295-5444
www.LifeMasteryBlog.com
www.LearnMastery.com

About the Author.........

Yanni Maniates, MS, CMI, is the founder of *The Life Mastery Institute.* I have been teaching Meditation, Intuitive Development, Healing, Spirituality and metaphysical subjects for the past twenty years. I have been meditating for the past forty years.

I am certified in Mediumship and numerous holistic and esoteric healing modalities. As well, I have published articles, book reviews, three Meditation CDs, numerous meditation and hypnotherapy cassettes and a number of certification programs.

I am also a contributor along with Zig Ziglar and Brian Tracy to *"101 Great Ways to Improve Your Life."* For more information see:

www.selfgrowth.com/greatways.html

The primary focus of all my work is to help people experience the "Embrace" and to listen to the "still small voice" within. I offer individual Intuitive Consultations, the Mentor with the Masters® Program, Spiritual Renewal Retreats, Intuitive Development and Meditation Classes and much more.

For testimonials about my work, please visit:

www.LearnMastery.com/About_Yanni_Maniates.htm

I have been happily married for the past 25 years to my soul mate Jaime. We are blessed with our wonderful son, Sean.

Jaime, Sean and Yanni Maniates

Web sites: *www.LifeMasteryblog.com*
www.LearnMastery.com

Remember...

Life <u>is</u> *Magical!*
and
Miracles are waiting for <u>you</u>!

You now have the Keys,
and all that is left
is for you to open the doors;
and there before you,
in all your splendor,
will You stand.

Yanni Maniates

Peace be with you!

The Magical Adventure continues......

A SPECIAL BONUS
MEDITATION BOOKLET
FOLLOWS!

MAGICAL KEYS
TO
SELF-MASTERY:

Creating Miracles in Your Life

Meditation Booklet

* Yanni Maniates *

Mentor with the Masters® Press

Table of Contents

Introduction

In order to help you to best integrate and absorb the message of *Magical Keys*, I have included four meditations that are based on ones I have outlined in the book.

By practicing these meditations or by just reading them to yourself, you will enter into the world of "peace and harmony." A world from which you can then manifest the miracles in your life that are there waiting for you.

Life is meant to be "magical." Claim the "magic" and the mystery of it all and then "live it!"

In this booklet I have included the full text of the four meditations so that you can either read them and absorb their energies, or, if you prefer, you can adapt them and record them in a way that works best for you.*

I know that you will enjoy the process of just "being present" with your Self. It is definitely the best and only way to "be."

Much Love and Many Blessings!

Yanni Maniates

---

* I have recorded these full-length meditations (forty-eight minutes worth). If you would like information about acquiring them, please email me at: yanni.maniates@verizon.net

---

MEDITATION ONE | Abdominal Breathing

This Meditation is an extended version of the one described in Chapter 1, *Peace of Mind is a Breath Away.*

Close your eyes and start by setting a clear intention that you want to spend quiet, quality time with yourself. Sit on a straight backed chair with your spine comfortably upright, but without being rigid or tense. Let your feet be firmly on the floor. Or, if you have the flexibility, by all means, sit in the traditional yoga posture on the floor. You can achieve a very profound state either way.

Now relax your jaw. Let it be slightly open. Let your shoulders drop and your arms be relaxed and place your hands on your thighs or in your lap.

Now begin by taking three, deep, cleansing, healing, relaxing breaths and start to really, really let go... Let each breath relax your body, your emotions and your mind. Just let go! When you are done with the three deep breaths, come back to a normal pattern of breathing.

Now while breathing in and out of your nostrils, focus your attention on your abdomen. Let your belly comfortably expand on the inhalation and contract on the exhalation. Don't strain. Be as relaxed as possible. Don't force a change in your breathing pattern in order to expand your abdomen; I'm not asking you to change anything, just notice the rise and fall of your abdomen. Breathing in, the abdomen expands slightly. Breathing out, exhaling, the abdomen contracts, slightly.

So just continue to be aware of your breath, of your breathing, your abdomen expanding, your abdomen contracting. Just have an awareness of your breath, your breathing.

If there are any distractions or noises that you might hear in the background or foreground, just ignore them. Any thoughts that may come to your mind now; just ignore them, they are not important. Or even any emotions that might bubble up; just ignore them, let them go, let yourself be still and let yourself be quiet.

Now as you do this, I would like you to count your breaths. See if you can count ten full breaths without getting lost in your thoughts. If you lose track, don't worry, just gently go back to counting your breaths again.

Count each inhalation and exhalation as one full breath. Do this for at least ten full breaths. By doing this a couple of times a day, you will begin to notice a major difference in how you feel.

Breathing in, breathing out, without getting lost in your thoughts, emotions or any distractions. Just be present within the stillness of yourself; for it is in that stillness that you will find the real you, that is, a human "being" and not a human "doing."

Continue counting your inhalations and your exhalations. If you lose count and don't make it to ten, that's fine. Start again and start counting all over again.

Some thoughts or emotions may make it into your awareness as you do this, but just ignore them and keep counting your breath. Just do you best to keep your primary awareness on your breath. Allow everything else to fade away, to recede.

If you get to ten, then just continue counting beyond the ten, just counting the breath, keeping your focus on your abdomen. When you focus on your abdomen and count your breath, it helps to calm you down. It draws the energies down that are bouncing around in your head and grounds them in your belly so to speak. Just breathe in and breathe out and note the rise and fall of your abdomen as you do.

As you continue, you might even notice or feel that your breathing has become deeper and slower. Your blood pressure is going down and your pulse is slowing. You are releasing relaxation hormones into your blood stream.

Physiologically you have made a significant change in your blood chemistry in just these few minutes. Whereas before you may have been in a fight or flight state and your body was tense and poised to run or attack and filled with stress hormones, now you are in a relaxed state, a peaceful state, a healing state. Continue the counting of the breath, the inhalation and the exhalation for a few more breaths....

And now you can begin to let go of your focus on your breath... now begin to become aware of your feet, your abdomen, your chest, your hands, your head, your breathing and your breath. Take a few conscious breaths and begin to come up and out. When you are ready you can begin to open your eyes, with a soft focus, so much more relaxed, so much more at peace, than when we began.

| Breathing Meditations to
Master Stress:
Emotional Distress
Feeling Overwhelmed
Mental Tension

This Meditation is an extended version of the one described in Chapter 3, *Using Meditation to Relax and Mange Stress.*

So close your eyes now and get nice and comfortable. Begin by taking three deep, cleansing, relaxing, healing breaths at your own pace. And with each breath you are relaxing your body, your emotions, and your mind. Each breath is bringing you into place of quiet, of calm, of healing, of wholeness, of light, of embrace, of peace. When you are done with the three deep breaths come back to a normal pattern of breathing. There is no where to go, nothing to do, nothing to think about. Just be! Be here now with yourself.

Begin now to bring your focus of attention to your breath. Be aware of your breath. You are not changing it yet. You are just aware of the rhythm of your breath, of your breath coming in through the nostrils and of the breath coming out of your nostrils. Notice that your breath causes the rise of your abdomen on the inhalation and a slight contraction of your abdomen on the exhalation.

The breath is such a gift. It is the rhythm of the flow of life within us. It connects us to our bodies, to our feelings, to our souls, to All That Is. Breathing in and breathing out. It is so simple. Peace of mind is just a breath away, a peaceful breath, a full breath, a healing breath, a whole breath. Continue now by placing your full attention on your abdomen's rising and falling.

It is in the abdominal area where you carry emotional stress. Use this breath to calm you self when you are overly excited, worried, anxious, or about to do something new.

And so breathe consciously into this area now. Just breathe in on your next inhalation. Breathe for a count of four. As you do, just allow your belly to expand, slightly more than it was a moment ago, but without strain. If there is any strain, then just let go. Don't strain at all. Then hold for a count of one or two. Then just imagine any tension or tightness or redness or irritation or inflammation in this area of the abdomen being gathered on that hold of the breath. And on the exhalation it just releases, it comes out. Breathe in through the nose and out through the nose.

So, do at least ten of these breaths. You breathe in and the abdomen expands or enlarges a bit, but without strain. Then hold for a count of one or two. You imagine, sense, see any tension or tightness being gathered and then you see it being expelled with the exhalation. The exhalation can be as long or short as you wish it to be.

You can, if it helps, visualize a gray haze gathering in your abdomen as you hold your breath and then it releases or dissipates as you exhale. Or you can use whatever imagery you want. Or just focus on counting your inhalation and exhalation and try to do ten of these breaths without having your mind get distracted by any thoughts or emotions.

Just know that as you are doing this, the stress hormones in your blood stream are gradually and totally disappearing in just three minutes. And in their place you are allowing your body now to release relaxation or calming and healing hormones. Literally you are bathing every cell in your body with health by taking these breaths.

Continue breathing into the abdominal area, releasing the emotional stress. Note that you are not only relieving the stress that you had from your day, but you are also gradually releasing stress that has been in this area for years. Each deep breath releases some. Each deep breath opens you to softening, to opening your heart, to quieting your mind, softening, softening, releasing, relaxing, letting go, letting go; breathing in for a count of four, holding for a count of one or two. Then just releasing for whatever count feels right.

No stress. If it feels stressful then just step back and be light. Be easy. Be free. Be innocent like a child again. Play! This is play not work. No one is grading you. Just be you, being with you, using a technique to quiet the mind and open the heart. Continuing now, continuing now with this deeper breath and with your abdomen rising and falling.....

Now I would like you to bring your attention to your chest area. This is where the tension lodges when you feel under pressure, overwhelmed, overworked, overloaded, suppressed, depressed. These energies get stuck in the chest area, the lungs, and the heart. As well, lack of confidence, fear, an excessive workload, family crisis, financial pressures get stuck in the chest area, the lungs, and the heart.

So, as you breathe now, your belly is still expanding and contracting, but now your focus is on your chest. You breathe in for a count of four and focus on the chest; then hold for a count of one or two, noticing any tension or tightness or negativity being gathered on the holding, then releasing it all on the exhalation. This is all rhythmic, gentle, and loving. It is like you are giving yourself an internal massage. Lovingly, tenderly, each cell is being stimulated into wholeness. Each cell is receiving the oxygen that gives it life and that gives it health. Breathing in and breathing out, so simple. Peace of mind but a breath away.

Each breath is a new beginning. Each inhalation brings in the new, the fresh, and the joyful. Each exhalation releases the old, the worn, and the stagnant. The breath is such a phenomenal gift, breathing in and breathing out. As you focus on the chest, the abdomen is still rising and falling, the chest releasing, relaxing, the heart opening, the lungs expanding, every muscle, every cell releasing and relaxing. Each in breath is new and fresh. Each exhalation is releasing the old.

Each moment, each breath is fresh and new. Each moment is a new beginning. Each breath is a new beginning. Breathing in and breathing out, the gift of the breath, the gift of life.

You are gifting yourself your own presence, just being present with yourself, with your body, with your breath, leaving behind any troubling emotions or thoughts or experiences, just being in the present, being in the presence of yourself. Breathing in and breathing out. Breathing in and breathing out, the gift of the breath.

As you continue, you may notice your breath getting deeper, the abdomen warming and the chest warming. If not, that's OK; these are all indications of the breath going deeper, of the oxygen being received, of the healing occurring. Breathing in and breathing out...

Continue with these deep breaths and now focus your attention on your head and your nostrils. Again the abdomen is rising and the chest expanding, but your focus in on the breath coming in the nostrils and as you do, imagine that it is going into your head and filling your head, every cell in this beautiful brain, this mind of yours that performs such miraculous functions is being fed the oxygen that it deserves, every cell.

Breathe in for a count of four, hold for a count of one or two, releasing any tensions or tightness. See it as a visual. Imagine it, intend it, whatever works for you. Stay in this breath, this rhythm of healing, of a new beginning. Inhaling and exhaling.

Again the abdomen continues to rise as the chest continues to expand. The focus is on the nostrils, the breath coming in, the head being filled, the brain being filled, the jaw being relaxed and open, the optical nerves being relaxed, the eyes relaxing, the ears relaxing, the neck relaxing, the throat relaxing. Breathing in and breathing out. Breathing in, holding for a count of one or two, finding your own rhythm and then releasing.

This is about you finding your own rhythm, that internal, eternal rhythm, the ebb and the flow of the breath, the rhythm of the heart, the rhythm of the breath, the rhythm of connection, the rhythm of life. Breathing in and breathing out, remembering that each new inhalation could be a new beginning. Leave behind the old and the stagnant, the past. And step into the present. Each new in breath brings you freshness and life and light and wholeness. Each out breath releases the old. Breathing in and breathing out, so simple, yet so deep, so profound, so transforming.

Continue on your own now and choose whichever of the three areas of your body we just did that you wish to focus on, whatever is right for you now. Knowing that anytime you wish during the day you can bring in this breath. There are moments or times of quiet, of being alone in your day. And you can breathe consciously. Every time you do, it will get better. Every time you do, it will help you to remember to do it more and more, and even when you forget, it will just kick in for you. Be present with yourself, with your breath.

I will go quiet now for a moment or two and allow you to be on your own. When you hear my voice again it will not startle you, you will actually go even deeper…

Know that the peace you have experienced just now is your natural state of being. It is your birthright. It is old programming that has taught you otherwise. But if you wish you can begin anew, each breath, each moment a new beginning, each breath, each moment, new and fresh. You can learn to practice peace, to be at peace, to be free...

Begin now to become aware of the chair that you are sitting on. Become aware of your physical body, how and where it touches the chair you are sitting upon, the placement of your feet and your hands. Now feel your torso, feel your head, feel your breath again. And then just begin at your own pace in your own way with a soft focus to very slowly, very gradually begin to open your eyes. So much more relaxed, so much more at peace. So much freer, healthier, than when we began, gradually beginning to come up, gradually beginning to open your eyes.

| # Creating the Experiences and Qualities You Want in Your Life

This Meditation is an extended version of the one described in Chapter 4, *Life is a Trip, But Where are You Going?*

Close your eyes and get nice and comfortable. Focus your attention on your breathing. And just observe the air as it comes in and as it goes out. Feel the breath as it comes in and, at your own pace, as it goes out. If your mind wanders just bring its focus back to the breath, the breathing...

As you breathe in on your next inhalation just notice that your stomach rises and your ribs expand a bit and even your collar bones rise slightly; and on the exhalation just let go all the air without strain and then notice, too, that your stomach contracts slightly.

Again just be aware of the mechanics of your breath. That is all you are doing right now – your stomach rises or expands on the inhalation. Again don't exaggerate this. Your ribs will expand a bit, as well. Even your collar bones rise as you fill your lungs naturally, slowly and fully. As you exhale you release the air from your lungs with ease, letting it all go, letting it all go, leaving room for your next inhalation.

Again, feel the mechanics of the breath, the stomach rising, the chest expanding, the collar bone area also rising and filling. Follow your own pace, not mine. And then empty your lungs, letting all the air out and letting the belly compress slightly. You are not pushing or straining with any of this, just letting it happen, letting it all go.

Now, I would like you to continue focusing on your breath, but in a different way. Imagine on your next inhalation that you are breathing in the attribute or quality of health, breathing in health. And on the exhalation you are releasing stress and distress, so breathing in health and releasing/exhaling stress and tension.

A color may appear with the breath coming in and perhaps a different color may also appear with the breath going out. Or maybe an image may appear for you or perhaps it will be just the words or a vibration, breathing in health, releasing stress and tension. Continue breathing in health and releasing stress and tension for at least seven full breaths...

Now just imagine that on your next inhalation you are inhaling peace and releasing anxiety, inhaling peace, exhaling anxiety, inhaling peace, exhaling anxiety. Feel that peace just filling you to overflowing. And then feel as that flows over, that the anxiety just releases from you. Again just breathing in peace, and exhaling anxiety. Peace of mind is but a breath away, an image away, a thought away, breathing in peace, exhaling anxiety. Continue breathing in peace and exhaling anxiety for at least seven full breaths...

On your next series of breaths, of inhalations and exhalations, I would like you to choose a quality you would like to embody, be it love, hope, confidence, etc. And following your own rhythm, breathe in the quality... Breathe in the quality so that each cell of your being is filled with this quality, this nature, this experience. By bringing in this quality or nature, you are releasing that which is its opposite and creating a healing for your self. Continue for at least seven full breaths...

And as you continue this process, your physical, mental, emotional and spiritual bodies are getting brighter and clearer. You are releasing the old, the stagnant, and the worn energies. Allowing for the new, the fresh, the joy filled to fill you to overflowing.

Remember to always fill yourself up for it is in that state of being full that one can truly give. It is also from that state that one can truly receive. Breathing in and breathing out, the rhythm of life. Each moment, each breath is fresh and new. Peace of mind is a breath away, a thought away, an image away.

Remember that health, love, peace are but a breath away, an image away, a thought away, hope, freedom, strength, courage, right there for the asking in each moment if we draw them in, if we ask for them. If we are open to receiving them.

Whatever qualities you wish to have, to become, to receive are there simply for the asking. Breathe it in and in breathing it in you can embody it and become it, you can integrate it and then you can release its opposite...

Now, let your breath come back to a normal, natural rhythm, breathing slowly, smoothly, deeply, steadily, easily, silently, allowing your self to feel peaceful and calm and relaxed.

Just continue now on your own, observing your breath. Observe as it comes in and as it goes out, the natural rhythm of the breath. If any thoughts that don't serve you come in, just ignore them. Continue choosing peace, choosing health, light and love, etc. They are all choices we can make each moment. Learn to choose what you experience.

You can learn to choose to be a master of your thoughts and your emotions and no longer be a victim of them. You have this freedom if you choose to exercise it. You can choose what you think about and what you feel and by doing so you are choosing what you get to experience in your life. You can be strong, free and unafraid! It is a choice you can make moment to moment...

Truly, how you feel and how you experience life are choices that *you* make each moment. The opportunity is always there for you to choose peace, to choose patience, to choose love, to choose acceptance, to choose trust, to choose courage, etc. They are always there for the asking.

I am now going to count from one to five and when I reach the number five you may open your eyes more relaxed and more at peace than when we began.

One! Two! Coming up slowly! Three – in a moment we will be at the number five at which time you may open your eyes, more relaxed, more at peace. Four! Five! Gradually beginning to open your eyes, more relaxed, more at peace, more at one with yourself than when we began.

| **"Being" the Child Within: A Meditation for Children (and Adults)**

This Meditation is an extended version of one of the meditations described in Chapter 5, *Meditating With Your Children*. It can be used by children and adults alike.

Begin by either sitting cross-legged on the floor in a yoga position or in a chair with your back comfortably erect. Close your eyes and breathe in and out through your nose slowly, counting to four on the in breath, then holding the breath for a count of one or so, and then exhaling for a count of four.

At you own pace and in your own way take just take about ten breaths like this as you allow yourself to go deeper and deeper, more and more relaxed... I am going to be quiet now for a moment or two as you take these ten deep breaths... Let each breath bring you deeper and deeper into a place of quiet and peace...

Now I'd like you to imagine that you are lying on a stack of cream-colored pillows while safely floating in a light blue boat on an emerald green lake. On each inhalation the boat rises slightly and on each exhalation it falls ever so gently. Coordinate your breathing with the image and sensation of floating in the boat. Do this, too, for another ten breaths or so...

Again, I am going to be quiet, so just continue with these very relaxing breaths and continue, as well, with the imagery of you lying safely, floating in the light blue boat, lying on a stack of crème colored pillows while the boats flows on an emerald green lake.

As well, notice as you do this that there is a clear blue sky above sprinkled occasionally with puffy white clouds floating by and that there is a refreshing summer breeze flowing through your hair. As well, just notice the fragrance, the sweet fragrance in the air.

Now, let go of this scene, let it shift. And imagine that you are now standing at the top of a staircase in your bare feet. The staircase is thickly carpeted in a color of your choice. Now begin by putting one foot down after the other as I slowly count you down 10.....9.....8..... going deeper and deeper 7.....6.....5..... going deeper and deeper 4.....3.....2 deeper and deeper and 1.

At the bottom of the staircase there is a door. Now open the door and walk inside, and as you do, you enter a beautiful, primeval forest and there you are drawn to a beautiful, majestic tree.

Take a deep breathe and go deeper. Now imagine that you are the tree, you are one with a tree. Feel that you are deep inside the center of a tree; the tree is your body. How does it feel? (pause) .... Now feel your roots burrowing deep into the earth. And just feel them going deeper and deeper (pause) ...., now feel the bark of the tree as part of your body; feel its texture and the protection it gives you; (pause)...., now feel the sap

running through you, just feel, don't think (pause) ....,
now feel all of the branches as part of you (pause) ....,
now feel all leaves as part of you (pause)...., now feel
the breeze gently rustling your leaves and the sun
warming you (pause)...., now feel a bird's nest in your
branches (pause).... Feel all of this wondrous life
running through you and around you (pause).....

Now just take a moment or two to "be" the tree. Allow
yourself to "be" the tree. Feel your "treeness." Feel
your strength! Feel your solidity and your connection
to the earth. Feel your breathing as a tree. Feel the sap
running throughout you in every way. Just "feel" what
it means to "be" "tree"...

And now just begin to let go of your connection to the
tree, knowing that you can come back anytime you
wish and feel the strength and solidity that the tree
symbolizes and brings to you.

Now gradually begin to come out of the meditation by
first focusing on your toes, then your feet, your calves,
your thighs, your torso, your hands, your head and
finally your breath.

Now when you are you can begin to open your eyes with a soft focus, so much more relaxed and at peace than when you began.